The Lost Wilderness

Rediscovering W.F. Ganong's New Brunswick

Nicholas Guitard

Edited by Alison Hughes.
Cover and page design by Chris Tompkins.
Front cover photo courtesy of the New Brunswick Museum (NBM, William Francis Ganong Collection, Image 1987-17-1218-145). Back cover photo by Nicholas Guitard.
Photographs by Nicholas Guitard except where noted.
Maps and archival photographs courtesy of the New Brunswick Museum (NBM) and the Provincial Archives of New Brunswick (PANB).
All images used by permission.
Printed in Canada.
10 9 8 7 6 5 4 3 2 1

Library and Archives Canada Cataloguing in Publication

Guitard, Nicholas, 1956-, author
The lost wilderness : rediscovering W.F. Ganong's New Brunswick / Nicholas Guitard.
Includes bibliographical references and index. Issued also in electronic formats.
ISBN 978-0-86492-877-1 (paperback).—ISBN 978-0-86492-834-4 (epub).
—ISBN 978-0-86492-835-1 (mobi)
1. Ganong, William F. (William Francis), 1864-1941.
2. Natural history—New Brunswick. 3. Natural history—New Brunswick
—Pictorial works. 4. Cartography—New Brunswick—
History—20th century. 5. New Brunswick—Geography. 6. Natural
History Society of New Brunswick. 7. Guitard, Nicholas, 1956- —
Travel—New Brunswick. 8. New Brunswick—Description and travel.
I. Title.
QH21.C3G84 2015   508.715'1   C2015-901872-2
                                              C2015-901873-0

We acknowledge the generous support of the Government of Canada, the Canada Council for the Arts, and the Government of New Brunswick.

Nous reconnaissons l'appui généreux du gouvernement du Canada, du Conseil des arts du Canada, et du gouvernement du Nouveau-Brunswick.

Goose Lane Editions
500 Beaverbrook Court, Suite 330
Fredericton, New Brunswick
CANADA E3B 5X4
www.gooselane.com

I dedicate this book to the late Dr. Gary Whiteford, PhD,
a kindred spirit in the pursuit of understanding and teaching
the works of William Francis Ganong.

It is too easy to forget how human
and natural history have always been intertwined.

— Karsten Heuer

Contents

Introduction

Photographing Ganong's New Brunswick

My interest in William Francis Ganong began while conducting research for my books on the waterfalls of New Brunswick. A 1908 paper on the morphology of New Brunswick waterfalls, one of Ganong's many reports to the Natural History Society of New Brunswick, caught my interest. It was my introduction to one of the province's most fascinating characters and began a personal quest to understand the gripping force that compelled him to explore New Brunswick.

As my research expanded from the Fredericton Public Library to the Legislative Library to the New Brunswick Museum in Saint John, I uncovered other fascinating Ganong monographs. I discovered that the importance of his work on the province's natural history was well understood by academics, and he was even named a Person of National Historic Significance in 1945. Yet the general public seemed to know little about the man, his writings, and the extraordinary scope of his field trips throughout the province. I decided that the best way for me and others to truly appreciate Ganong's comprehensive body of work was to follow him into the wilderness. I wanted to find the places he had mapped, sketched, and described in his field notes, and I needed to photograph them.

Ganong's field trips, research, and correspondence were extensive, and it was no small task to settle on which of these to document and include in

Adder Lakes Trip 1902

An excerpt from the notes written by William F. Ganong
of his 1902 field trip

North Branch Renous River, Northumberland County, August 2011

this book. I decided to travel to the locations that I found in his reports, in his friends' field notes, and in the photographs they took. His original pocket-sized notebooks are in the New Brunswick Museum, but age and difficult penmanship made them not very useful for my purpose. Instead, I relied on Natural History Society bulletins from 1882 to 1912 for his notes and maps, as well as field notes written by his companions Mauran Furbish and Arthur Pierce. By combining material from these sources, I was able to determine the intended routes of Ganong's field trips and their time sequence.

With the aid of current topographical maps and Google Earth, I pored over his hand-sketched maps and detailed reports to identify coordinates and potential routes to the sites. I attempted to find the exact locations where Ganong had stood when he conducted barometric readings to measure the height of a mountain or took a series of compass bearings to triangulate a location to a known reference point. As I read and re-searched, my resolve hardened. Every time I hiked through the forest to photograph a landscape or waterfall, I thought about this book. On several occasions, I questioned my motive in starting such an ambitious project, always coming back to the same conclusion: I had to satisfy my curiosity about William F. Ganong and see for myself the natural places that had so impressed and intrigued him.

I wanted to illustrate the breadth and reach of his trips, so I decided to include the field trips that I thought readers would find most interesting. As well, I have included some of the fascinating, and sometimes eccentric,

Dr. William Francis Ganong surveying from
summit of Chief's Mountain, Northumberland County, 1905

(NBM, William Francis Ganong Collection, Image 1987-17-1219-66)

vignettes that Ganong published as *Sundry Items*. His opinions on natural
phenomena in articles such as "The Fact Basis of the Fire (or Phantom) Ship
of Bay Chaleur" illustrate the diversity of his interests and provide further
insight into his personality. Photographing notable landscapes and features
that he had described was key to my project. As it turned out, some of the
most pleasurable places to photograph were the various canoe trips, in
particular the Restigouche River and upper section of the Nepisiguit River.
In many instances, I found that the appearance of the location had altered
since Ganong's time, either through natural changes or human intervention.

Unlike Ganong, I had to limit the time I took for research and travel, fully
understanding that there would always be the siren call of another place to
visit. I excluded Ganong's 1907 field trip in the Tobique River valley since
details of that watershed are included in Field Trip 6 in this book. As well,
I did not include excursions to the Dungarvan and Bartholomew Rivers or

Above: Looking west from
Mount Ganong towards
Mount Carleton Provincial
Park, Restigouche County,
June 2011

Left: Looking up
Patchell Brook Gorge,
Northumberland County,
May 2012

the excursions that followed his 1912 canoe trip down the Canaan River. A complete list of Ganong's field trips and the titles of his 138 monographs in the Natural History Society of New Brunswick bulletins are, however, in the appendices at the end of this book.

Like Ganong, I usually travelled with a friend or two for safety and companionship. With field notes, maps, GPS, compass, and, most importantly, my camera equipment, we tramped through dense forests, waded across brooks and streams, slogged through wet meadows, and scrambled down steep mountainsides to find the landscapes and features that Ganong documented. There were many memorable moments, such as when I stood with friends Rod O'Connell and Karl Branch on the crest of the mountain named for Ganong and gazed westward toward the encircling mountains that embraced the setting sun.

Heat and the inevitable black flies and mosquitoes made some memories less pleasant. An exhausting field trip to photograph the boulder scree that forms the south face of the ravine above Patchell Brook taught me about the grit and determination I would need to follow Ganong — and the need to choose the right season.

Timing was only one of many lessons that I learned as I worked to find and photograph the terrain and rivers Ganong explored and mapped. On occasion, I ventured out alone in search of several locations to photograph. My respect for the dogged determination he brought to his explorations increased, as did my appreciation for his love of the New Brunswick landscape. Ganong must have felt it was his responsibility to create a body of scientific work for future generations before the pristine wilderness was lost to the development he already saw encroaching. I believe he saw his maps and articles as an investment on behalf of the province of his birth. This book is my opportunity to tell others about William Francis Ganong, his amazing explorations, his contributions to the study of natural history, and his continuing importance to the province of New Brunswick.

Laying the Groundwork
William F. Ganong

In reviewing Dr. Ganong's life-work, it is very evident that the influences which were brought to bear on him in boyhood determined the trend of his future activities.[1]

For more than fifty years, William Francis Ganong spent most of his summers exploring the New Brunswick wilderness. He relished his adventures in the backwoods, hiking and paddling into often-unmapped areas in the pursuit of scientific knowledge. As professor of botany at Smith College in Northampton, Massachusetts, his job afforded him the time and financial means to follow his passion. It was during childhood, however, that he developed the love of nature and devotion to New Brunswick that led to his life's work.

Ganong was born on February 19, 1864, in what was then Carleton, NB, and is now West Saint John. When he was seven, his parents, James Harvey and Susan E. Brittain Ganong, moved with William and his six younger siblings to St. Stephen. There, James and his brother Gilbert established the Ganong Brothers candy factory. William was inspired by his family's interest in science and nature, especially during summer vacations at the family homestead in Springfield. He spent hours on excursions into the woods and along the shores of Belleisle Bay at the side of his grandfather, Francis D. Ganong. According to his sister, Susan B. Ganong, "he was an impressionable youth, eager to listen and learn." She attributed all her brothers' scientific curiosity to these family outings.

William Francis Ganong
at sixteen years of age
(PANB, Anne Ganong Seidler fonds P606-4)

Their grandfather, Francis D. Ganong, was devoted to the young boys and spent many hours with them, teaching them to swim, fish, handle a sailboat, drive horses and observe all forms of plant and animal life in that region. These vacations had no doubt a profound influence on the boys in creating the love of the out-of-doors and an interest in all living things. Their father James H. Ganong, was also a lover of the open spaces, and his scientific and philosophic turn of mind had its effect as well, as they accompanied him in many excursions to the woods.[2]

William had ample opportunity to observe all manner of flora and fauna and to develop the scientific interests that would inspire his later field trips. One of his earliest excursions without his father was a fishing trip with his uncles to Clinch Stream in the Musquash watershed in late June 1880.[3] Eager to join his uncles, he borrowed his grandfather's rather large boots, and by the time they reached camp, William was suffering from painful blisters. Even at the age of sixteen he treated the trip as a learning experience, and in this case, the lesson was less about science and more about life. His trip notes explain why he decided not to tell his parents all the details:

> *Did we gain or lose by our excursion? Were it not for one thing I would say most emphatically, we gained. That one thing is — we broke the Sabbath. For this reason I can never tell my folks about it without making them think how wicked I am. But that was no worse than lots of other things I have done on Sunday.*[4]

New Brunswick Museum founder Dr. J.C. Webster described his friend's education as follows:

The boy started life in circumstances similar to those experienced by the majority of New Brunswick boys, without special privileges or advantages of any kind, attending the public schools, as most have done, but unlike the experience of the majority of our youth he studied in a school, not registered in the Provincial Department of Education, viz, the great school of Nature.[5]

After distinguishing himself academically in high school, William attended the University of New Brunswick in Fredericton, receiving a bachelor's degree in 1884 and a master's degree in 1886. Throughout this time, he took part in summer field trips led by members of the Natural History Society of New Brunswick, whom he considered mentors. A voracious curiosity and an ability to listen intently endeared him to his elders and colleagues, prompting them to share their knowledge freely. Even as a student, his prolific output of articles for the society's bulletins distinguished him. His subjects went beyond natural history to the annals of First Nations and early Acadian settlers, and he studied the Maliseet and Mi'kmaq languages, as well as French and German.

After UNB, Ganong attended Harvard University, where he earned an applied baccalaureate degree in 1887 and became an assistant instructor in 1889. In 1888, he married Jean Carman,[6] a Fredericton girl, the sister of poet Bliss Carman and the cousin of author Sir Charles G.D. Roberts, whom Ganong later reviled for personifying nature. Ganong's thirst for knowledge next took him to the University of Munich, where he received a PhD in 1894, followed by the move to Smith College to teach botany. He was later appointed director of the college's botanical gardens, a position he held until his retirement in 1932.

Ganong's New Brunswick field trips took place almost every summer from 1882 until 1929, continuing throughout his years in the United States. As his age increased and his health declined, the trips became shorter. Yet, with the aid of an automobile, he was still able to visit several locations in a single summer with seemingly undiminished enthusiasm. In the summer of 1915, for example, he travelled upriver from Fredericton to the Shogomoc and Pokiok streams to determine if the physiographic nature of either would support his premise about the preglacial course of the Saint John River. From there, he travelled overland to the headwaters of the Magaguadavic and Digdeguash Rivers to complete field studies begun several years earlier. He then went north for a hasty exploration of the

Ganong's car on the Shepody Road, Kings County, 1920

(NBM, William Francis Ganong Collection, Image 1987-17-1225-37)

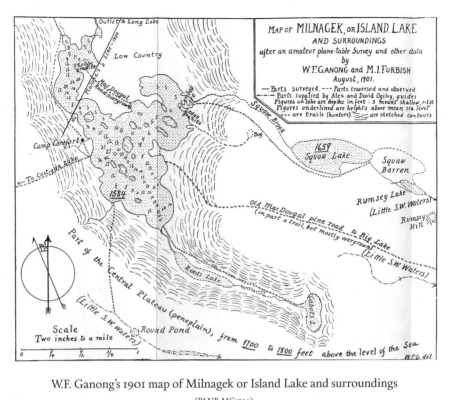

W.F. Ganong's 1901 map of Milnagek or Island Lake and surroundings
(PANB-MC1799)

Tetagouche and Jacquet Rivers. That same summer, he also travelled up the Nepisiguit River to its confluence with Gordon Brook and the start of the ancient Nepisiguit–Miramichi portage trail via Portage River. This route is as historically important to New Brunswick as the Cains-Gaspereau portage described in Field Trip 15 of this book.

Ganong always treated his field trips as serious scientific excursions, undertaken with little regard for either financial rewards or honours. His Natural History Society articles between 1884 and 1917 reflect an incredibly broad range of interests from cartography and botany to physical geography and even an English translation of *Voyages to Acadia and New England* from the original French of Samuel de Champlain. It is generally accepted that Ganong began the serious geographic study of New Brunswick and the Maritime provinces. Later in life, he started to write a definitive geography of New Brunswick, but he destroyed it when he realized that failing health would prevent its completion.

W.F. Ganong mapping Holmes Lake, Northumberland County, 1901

(NBM, William Francis Ganong Collection, Image 1987-17-1218-145)

Clear-cut on the Southwest Miramichi River, York County, May 2008

At the time of Ganong's field trips, large tracts of New Brunswick had not yet been surveyed or scientifically studied, and his monographs provided the first glimpse of the province's interior. He was exploring before the onset of road construction that opened the wilderness areas to industry and recreation. The province's vast network of ponds, lakes, and rivers provided the primary transportation routes. Woodsmen and professional guides had established hunting and trapping lines, and geologists such as Professor Loring W. Bailey had undertaken survey work on behalf of the federal and provincial governments. Yet few others ventured into the wilderness regions, and many mountains and lakes were not even officially named. This was largely due to the extreme difficulty of accessing the areas, but as the New Brunswick Museum's curator of botany, Stephen Clayden, noted: "His physical energy was no less prodigious than his intellectual drive."[7]

In 1898, Ganong wrote about the lack of a unified topographical map system, suggesting that it would be an investment that would pay back dividends in the development of the province. Meanwhile, he systematically mapped the physiographic characteristics of the areas he visited.

He reproduced and enhanced many earlier maps and gained considerable renown among Canada's elite mapmakers.

Ganong turned New Brunswick into his laboratory, interpreting the world around him through scientific reasoning and fact-based observation. He strove to understand the science behind natural phenomena from the formation of waterways to the coloration of rivers, and he strongly believed that the better such matters were understood, the further advanced society would become.

He challenged his colleagues and government representatives to venture into the wilderness in pursuit of scientific discovery and better stewardship of the province's natural resources. His observations and research revealed problems with forestry practices, and he urged government officials to develop a forestry management policy, claiming:

> *The greatest natural source of wealth of New Brunswick lies in her forests. These are steadily deteriorating. The public is uninformed and hence indifferent as to their fate. These three facts constitute a forestry problem of the gravest character, and one vastly important to the future of this province.* [8]

Together with long-time friend J.C. Webster, Ganong was instrumental in the development of the New Brunswick Museum in Saint John. Curator Stephen Clayden notes that Ganong's studies were motivated in part by his recognition of the need to preserve the rapidly disappearing evidence of New Brunswick's past. He searched for the exact location of historic events and corresponded with numerous colleagues, refining his knowledge of historic sites and First Nations nomenclature. His work also encompassed archaeology, and his contribution on the excavation of a prehistoric shell midden at Bocabec in Charlotte County is considered a seminal archaeological study. The study, led by George F. Matthew marked the beginning of systematic, scientific examinations of shell-bearing archaeological sites in Canada. Ganong believed his work would improve understanding of the province's unique connections between people and place.

When William F. Ganong died in 1941, Canada lost a great scientist and scholar. No one before or since has studied the natural and physiographic history of the province in such detail. Today, his observations and investigations into New Brunswick's human and natural history remain relevant. The articles he wrote, the maps he created, the artifacts he collected, and the impressive example of his commitment to exploration and research constitute a precious inheritance. His body of work is an important legacy for the people of New Brunswick, one we should all be grateful for and never take for granted. The following is a tribute to him and to the place where his work began, the New Brunswick wilderness.

FIELD TRIPS

1

Learning to Lead

St. Croix River and Passamaquoddy Bay, Summer 1882

> The objects of quest in these journeys while primarily scientific, have been secondarily historical, especially as to facts which link man with places.
>
> — S. CLAYDEN[1]

During his summer breaks from the University of New Brunswick, Ganong undertook field trips with other students and some of his siblings. Always taking advantage of an opportunity to learn, he used these early field trips to hone the planning and leadership skills that were central to the success of his later excursions into the wilderness.

He also established the research methodology that he continued to use as he explored the province. Prior to a field trip, he would determine the First Nations or French origin of an area's name, locate original maps to understand the topology, and study any geological reports. Armed with this pertinent information, he would plan the travel route and camping logistics.

In the summer of 1882, Ganong's brother Edwin and friends Harry Wetmore and Samuel Kain joined the self-appointed captain and cook as he guided the intrepid group through a summer on the St. Croix (Chiputneticook) River system. Throughout the trip, the group stopped and camped along the river's eastern shore and examined the geology as well as the flora and fauna of the shoreline. During a storm, they camped on the banks of the St. Croix River opposite Dochet (St. Croix) Island where Sieur de Mons, cartographer Samuel Champlain (later changed to de Champlain), and seventy-nine men spent the winter of 1604. It's clear from Ganong's field notes that inclement weather didn't dampen his spirits, as he wrote:

The upper St. Croix River, June 2011

St. Croix (Dochet) Island from the Canadian Heritage Park,
Bayside, August 2011

We were quite comfortable except for a slight dampness in the quilts, the fire helped to keep up our spirits, and altogether we had not a bad night. Then outside in the lull of the storm, it was so still. We could see the revolving light on Dochet, casting its beams on the dark night.[2]

Largely because of the island's early history, the river had become part of the border between the United States and Canada in the 1783 Treaty of Paris, upheld in the Webster-Ashburton Treaty of 1842. This history fascinated Ganong, who was familiar with the river from previous excursions with his father. The information he gathered during these trips was used years later for the 300th anniversary celebration of the French explorers' winter on the island and its subsequent international importance. In his 1904 essay honouring the tercentenary, Ganong described the impact of St. Croix Island:

The island is one of those rare places where the thoughtful student may come into communion with the silent witness of history, and thereby experience that exaltation which comes to some at such times, as it does to others in the contemplation of beauty in nature or art, to others in the spirit of literature, to others in the triumph of scientific discovery.[3]

Ganong and his friends sailed down the lower end of the river to Passamaquoddy Bay, passing through the Western Channel between Saint Andrews and Navy Island and into Chamcook Harbour. They ventured inland and climbed both Chamcook and Greenlaw Mountains to gain a better understanding of the region. Ganong wrote of the view, describing "a panorama of sea and shore, lake and forest, island and river."[4] Once in Chamcook Harbour, Ganong explored the islands and shoreline and documented the various invertebrates he found. He included this data in a report to the Natural History Society entitled "The Zoology of the Invertebrate Animals of Passamaquoddy Bay." He noted the abundance of common clams, writing:

Filling every available locality where there are flats of fine sand and mud, there is probably not a single mile of coast on the Bay where they do not occur, their presence at any point being shown by the dead shells thrown up by the tide and by the little holes out of which they send a tiny stream of water from their siphons when disturbed.[5]

Clam flats on the Minister's Island causeway at low tide,
Saint Andrews, July 2011

Beyond botanical and zoological studies, Ganong also spent time on
archaeology. The group explored an old First Nations encampment on
Minister's Island, taking time to note and map the location of artifacts to
help explain their importance to New Brunswick history before heading
farther east to Frye Island. Unconstrained by today's laws, they also collected archaeological items for later study and display, noting: "we found a
rock with a great number of lines across each other, and looking as though
made by some sharp instrument. Our specimens were brought back to the
tent with great delight."[6]

I made several road trips to Charlotte County to photograph the upper
St. Croix River and locations in and around Saint Andrews. I also made it
a point to visit the gravesite of Ganong.

2

Science and History

*Squatook Region of Quebec, Madawaska River,
and Upper Saint John River, Summer 1885*

Just now the wind is blowing through the trees outside,
and an occasional gust shakes the tent, but inside is very
comfortable, blanket-carpeted and candle lighted.

— W.F. GANONG[1]

The summer before he entered Harvard University, Ganong travelled
north by train to Edmundston with friend Samuel W. Kain. From there,
they followed the Madawaska River into Quebec and the mountainous
region of Gaspé around Lake Temiscouata. The large lake was once part
of the principal portage route from the St. Lawrence River to the Saint
John River and the Bay of Fundy. The primary focus on this trip, however,
was to the east, studying the physiography of the Squatook chain of lakes
to find a lesser-known portage.

Ganong had information concerning the Lake Temiscouata portage and
the Squatook portage from an amateur historian, the Reverend William
Raymond. From the western side of the lake the two young men canoed
northeast and went up the Touladi River and through a series of smaller
lakes to Squatook Lake before hiking to the top of Squatook Mountain.
From the summit, Ganong verified that a chain of interconnected streams
and bogans reached southward back to the Madawaska River via Beardsley
Brook as well as locating the headwaters of the Green River. Armed with the
sketches he made and some rough maps, they found the portage route from
the last lake in the chain and made their way back to the Madawaska River.

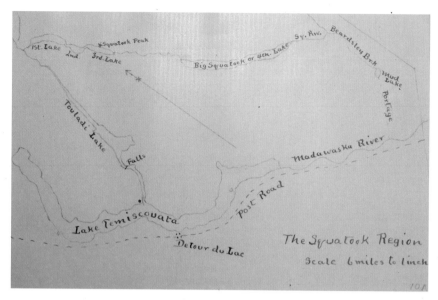

W.F. Ganong's 1885 map of the Squatook Region, Gaspé, Quebec
(NBM, William Francis Ganong Collection)

Ganong and Kain returned to Edmundston content with their work and began the long canoe trip down the Saint John River to Fredericton. Just above Saint-Léonard, they ventured up the Grand River to study its relationship to the Saint John and Restigouche watersheds before continuing downriver to Grand Falls. There, Ganong studied and recorded salient features of the falls and gorge. This information would later become part of his Natural History Society report on the morphology of New Brunswick waterfalls, which classified six different types in the province, with examples. He categorized Grand Falls as a glacial fall, formed in the last ice age when a large piece of glacial debris blocked the natural path of a river and forced it to rush around, eventually forming a gorge. Ganong and Kain spent a few days in Grand Falls before portaging their canoe and supplies through the village to the bottom of the gorge and continuing down the Saint John. They stopped for the night at the mouth of the Rapide de Femme Stream, where it is very likely that they hiked the short distance to the spectacular high waterfall.

The following day, the friends camped at the confluence of the Saint John and the Aroostook Rivers and ventured up the Aroostook's narrow valley to the boundary between Canada and the United States. They stopped on the next day's paddle to study the geology of the Tobique River

Rapide de Femme falls, Victoria County, October 2008

narrows.[2] Back on the Saint John River, the companions canoed downriver to camp on an island just below the settlement at Bath. They paddled on through the days that followed, stopping at points of interest such as the narrow gorge of the Pokiok Stream and an ancient Maliseet portage route leading to the Penobscot watershed. Ganong also began a preliminary study of the upper Saint John River that later led to his assumption about its formation. The two men parted in Fredericton, and Ganong returned to St. Stephen to continue the archaeological work on Frye Island that he had started in 1881.

Ganong's 1885 observations on the physiography of the Saint John River became the genesis of a categorization system for ancient rivers. It also helped him to realize the immense influence geography had on early settlement patterns. He rarely revisited the upper Saint John River on later field trips, intentionally avoiding populated areas to focus his attention on the vast, unmapped interior of the province. He returned in 1892 to conduct further fieldwork at Lake Temiscouata, noting its physiographic relationship to the Kedgwick River and the Restigouche and developing a theory about the ancient path of the Saint John River. He also revisited the Madawaska region once more in 1919 to explore the Green River.

3

Romantic and Picturesque

Restigouche River, Summer 1896

New Brunswick is a land of splendid rivers. I have looked on
the maps in vain for an equal extent of country elsewhere
which can show so fine a series.

— W.F. Ganong[1]

In the summer of 1896, Ganong joined fellow Natural History Society
member George Upham Hay, a mentor and one of New Brunswick's foremost botanists, for a canoe trip on the Restigouche River. Over a period
of twelve days, they documented the river's flora and physiography. In a
report to the society, Hay described the fulfillment of his long-deferred
hope of exploring the wilderness region and the unparalleled beauty of
the Restigouche. "With an appetite sharpened by twelve years of wait-
ing, I became a willing partner in last summer's excursion," Hay wrote,
remembering:

> *a most delightful trip, in almost un-interrupted fine weather, and
> upon a river that has no superior in romantic and picturesque scenery,
> even in this province of beautiful rivers. I feel sure that this, the first
> descriptive account of the flora of the Restigouche, will be full of
> interest to you, occupying as this river does, the northern limit of
> the province, and prior to the visit of Dr. Cox and Mr. Brittain, a
> few years ago, almost unknown to botanists.[2]*

George Upham Hay writing field notes, 1896

(NBM, William Francis Ganong Collection, Image 1987-17-1218-129)

Ganong's typical list for field trips

(NBM, William Francis Ganong Collection, F454-33)

The flora may not have been known, but by the middle of the 1800s, the Restigouche River and its tributaries were widely regarded as prime salmon-fishing waters. Private lodges, destinations of the rich and famous, dotted the river valley, the riparian rights largely reserved for use by their members. Further up along the Kedgwick and Gounamitz Rivers, vast tracts of forest were being harvested, and the timber floated downriver to sawmills at Atholville and Campbellton. Much of the Restigouche had been surveyed by 1886, and the two men made use of many forms of transport as they travelled into the northern plateau region that dominates the northwest part of the province.

At the end of a long train journey from Saint John up the Saint John River Valley to the settlement at Saint-Léonard, Ganong and Hay gathered supplies, acquired a canoe, and hired guides and a wagon.

The Gounamitz River,
Restigouche County, May 2009

Then they began the trip up into the low, sweeping hills along the valley of the Grand River and away from the Saint John River valley. For the first few hours, the wagon trip was enjoyable, but they soon endured rough hauling roads that finally disappeared completely. "The last or frontier settlement is on the verge of civilization," Hay wrote, "and we are standing before the last hut before plunging into the forest."[3]

The forest stretched east and west, and small lakes nestled in the highlands, the headwaters for five tributaries of the Restigouche. The rivers cut narrow valleys through and along the mountains, carving deeper as they descend towards the main river and eventually to the Bay of Chaleur. One anomaly, the Southeast Branch of the Upsalquitch River, runs through a narrow chasm in a fault zone, and Ganong later returned to study this formation. Hay's report described the Central Highlands plateau. "This watershed, dividing the St. John from the Restigouche," he wrote, "is a gently undulating tableland, elevated about eight hundred or a thousand feet above sea-level and well watered."[4]

On foot, and with the help of the guides, they reached the headwaters of Hunter Brook. From there, the group pushed the canoe down the brook through heavy brush and deadfalls to emerge at its confluence with the Little Main Restigouche River. They explored the rocky gorge and

The Little Main Restigouche, above the
confluence of the Kedgwick River, June 2011

documented various ferns before settling for the night. A river teeming
with trout provided their evening meal after a long, demanding day. The
following day, the guides headed back to Saint-Léonard, and Ganong and
Hay canoed down to the first major tributary, the Gounamitz River. They
set up camp on a sandbar at the base of a cliff and learned a valuable lesson.
Ganong noted in his journal: "this was a mistake as we had a bad night of
it with the midges and mosquitoes which allowed little sleep."[5]

Ganong and Hay spent their days documenting flora along the river,
working in peaceful silence except for the sound of their own canoe pad-
dles. Since this upper part of the watershed was difficult to access and
largely unused, they encountered no one until they reached a small farm at
the confluence with the Kedgwick River. Other than the seasonal fishing
camps, it was the only human habitation they saw before arriving at Mann
Settlement, just below the confluence with the Upsalquitch River. Ganong
took every opportunity to continue his studies of the French settlers and
their language, and he was impressed by their fortitude in carving out a
living in this wilderness region.

The abundant forest growth in this area, a wealth of balsam fir, pine,
and several species of hardwood, particularly impressed Hay. He noted
that the river was "flanked by hills rising very steep from waters' edge,

Looking down the Upsalquitch River towards Squaw Cap, August 2013 and 1896

(Bottom: NBM, William Francis Ganong Collection, Image 1987-17-1218-203)

but scarcely ever too steep not to admit of luxuriant vegetation, chiefly evergreen."[6]

For Ganong, the physiography and geological formations along the Restigouche River provided little in the way of interesting phenomena. He described it as having a "comparatively simple, though not uneventful history."[7] Through fieldwork and subsequent research, he determined that the river was relatively new, geologically speaking, in comparison with its tributaries. He speculated that the headwaters of the Kedgwick and Gounamitz Rivers had at one time turned away from the Rimouski and Saint John Rivers respectively to become tributaries of the Restigouche. He noted that the main river itself was ancient and well-defined, a gentle meandering waterway with long, sweeping turns, its course guided by lofty ridges more than six hundred feet in elevation. At Cross Point, these rock ramparts forced the river to turn almost 360 degrees back on itself before returning to follow its original direction. Hay's report describes this unique feature:

> *Cross Point is a romantic spot on this most picturesque part of the river. Climbing to the top of the rocky and dizzy height, which is surmounted by a rough wooden cross, we overlook a magnificent stretch of endless hills and gorges. Three hundred feet below us the river flows in a northeast direction and curving round, forming an oval peninsula, takes a directly opposite course. So closely does the river double on itself that one can sit on the narrow mountain ledge, about the width of a saddle, with a foot dangling over each section.*[8]

Further downriver, near the confluence of the Upsalquitch River, the peak of Squaw Cap appeared above the treetops. Ganong and Hay set out on foot to a nearby settlement at Robinsonville to meet Joseph Harris, their guide for a hike to the summit of Squaw Cap, the highest peak along the Restigouche River. On the ascent, they identified several rare species of ferns and collected some unusual flowering plants, including an orchid unknown to both botanists. Looking from the summit, they could identify Bald Peak and Sagamook to the south on the Tobique River.

The Restigouche trip helped motivate Ganong to measure systematically the height of most of the mountains in New Brunswick, as well as to determine the elevation of lakes and other points of geographical interest.

The Restigouche, looking upriver from Bulls Head Rock,
Restigouche County, June 2011

In a later report to the Natural History Society, he pointed out that very
little was known about the exact elevation of the province's highest points:

> *In the summer of 1896, I climbed two of the best-known and
> most accessible of the higher hills of the province — Squaw Cap,
> in Restigouche, and Mount Pleasant in Charlotte. Later I sought
> information about their heights, but found, with surprise, that for
> neither was it accurately known; and later inquiry showed that
> this is true as to the heights of most New Brunswick hills. Indeed,
> nobody knows positively where the highest point in New Brunswick
> lies, much less how high it is.*[9]

As Ganong and Hay canoed downriver toward their destination in Atholville,
they observed a striking difference between the colour of the water in
the Restigouche River and that in one of its tributaries, the Matapedia.
Ganong noted that "the Restigouche is light green and the Matapedia light
brown; and where these two come together, one may run a canoe for three
hundred yards on a boundary so sharp that on the right all is clear green
and on the left all equally clear brown."[10] Later, after analyzing maps of the
headwaters, he speculated that this colour difference was the result of the

Restigouche forming in the mountainous highlands, while the Matapedia originated in a series of wetlands in the Gaspé. He and Hay spent some time in Atholville, studying the local flora and land formations, before boarding the Intercolonial railway for the long trip back to Saint John.

Today, a century of forestry has changed the makeup of the Restigouche watershed. Large tracts of land have been clear-cut to the edges of the lofty hills, while the previously mixed forest has been turned into a monoculture of black spruce. These changes have made the river susceptible to sudden fluctuation in water levels after heavy rainfalls. Nevertheless, the river waters are still clear and cold, fed by the many springs and lakes hidden in the thick woods, and the Restigouche River system still provides some of New Brunswick's most beautiful scenery.

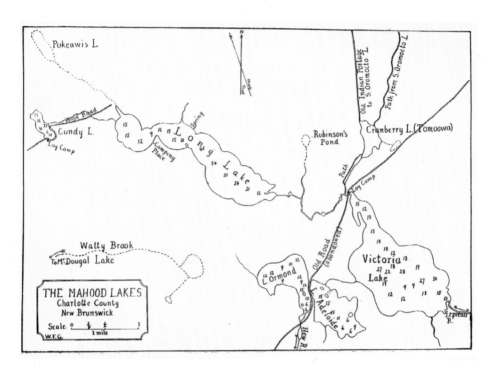

W.F. Ganong's 1898 map of the Mahood Lakes

(PANB-MC1799)

4

A Sense of Adventure

Mahood (Lepreau) Lakes
and the Lepreau River, Summer 1897[1]

Because of his scrupulous honesty and his engrained passion
for accuracy, all his contributions bear an impress which gives
them an enduring value.

— J.C. WEBSTER[2]

To accomplish any worthwhile goal requires steadfast determination, a
quality that Ganong had in abundance. Beyond his overwhelming scientific
curiosity, he possessed a great sense of adventure and amazing stamina. Few
rivers in the province that carry a similar volume of water are as difficult
to canoe as the Lepreau River in southwestern New Brunswick, but in the
summer of 1897, Ganong and three companions travelled the length of the
river, documenting the physiographic character of the Mahood (Lepreau)
Lakes and the Lepreau River.

The trip began easily enough. They travelled from St. George up along
the Magaguadavic River to McDougall Lake, where Ganong spent a day
completing research he had begun two years earlier, then portaged the
canoes via an old hauling road to the Lepreau Lakes. They walked through
rolling, granite hills, sloping gently towards the Bay of Fundy, near the
height of land between the Lepreau watershed and the Oromocto and
Magaguadavic watersheds. The terrain still bore the scars of the forest
fires that roared through the region after the infamous Saxby Gale of 1869.
Ganong described the landscape throughout the area as arid and desolate.
"The very soil has been burnt and washed away," he noted, "and nothing

The shallows of Victoria Lake, Charlotte County, July 2012

shows but the bare granite boulders."[3] One positive effect of this open landscape was that it allowed him to climb the hills easily, to take elevation measurements, and to triangulate distant hills without obstruction.

Concerned about the lack of scientific information and detailed maps, they spent several days canoeing the perimeter of the lakes, taking compass readings, documenting interesting features, and measuring the lakes' depth. Ganong's field notes suggest the trip's value lay in the data collected rather than in the discovery of any significant features:

> *At the head of the Lepreau River lies a chain of small lakes known to a few fishermen but hitherto unvisited by any naturalist. I spent two weeks — July 10th-24th — on the lakes and river, and although found little of interest, it is nevertheless, some satisfaction to know just what kind of a country it is from the scientific standpoint.*[4]

Ganong speculated about the cause of formations such as the beaches on the western edge of Victoria Lake, noting that "its shores are of the typical boulder sort, but on the west and southwest occurs much attractive white sand beach, which has no doubt been derived by wave and ice action from the ridge of sand and gravel along the western side."[5] He decided that

Lepreau Falls, Lepreau River, December 2012

glacial debris had dammed the original course of the river in several locations, creating the series of shallow lakes. Since the lakes could not drain
through their blocked outlets, they diverted to become the headwaters of
the Lepreau River, Musquash River, and New River.

With his friends, he started down the West Branch Lepreau from the
eastern tip of Victoria Lake, paddling in an easterly direction until joining
the North Branch Lepreau. This section of the river, repeatedly obstructed
by boulders and granite ledges, sloped quickly away from the lake. Covering
nine and half kilometres took two long days of the most severe labour, with
twenty portages along the rough, slippery riverbed. Below the confluence
the river quickened, and at Monson Falls the explorers were forced to line
their canoes through the rapids. When they reached Ragged Falls, they
had to portage once again.

Below the falls, the Lepreau widened to flow over a bed of fine, granu-
lar rock for several kilometres before reaching Keyhole Falls, a jumble of
boulders and granite where the river jammed through a narrow slot in
the granite bedrock. Long, angular quartz dykes stretched east to west
across the face of the falls. Below, the Lepreau River meandered towards
the Bay of Fundy, dropping over a series of steps before crashing into the
salt water in the most dramatic fashion.

Ragged Falls, Lepreau River, July 2012

It was during this and subsequent field trips to the coast that Ganong noticed an interesting difference between two distinct types of rivers that flow into the Bay of Fundy.

> On the one hand, those of the western series — the St. Croix, the Digdeguash, the Magaguadavic, New River, the Lepreau — all have falls where they meet the salt water, and, at least at high tide, fall directly into it from considerable heights. On the other hand, the eastern series, beyond Mispec, all run evenly into the sea without natural falls.[6]

He attributed this to the preglacial height of the mountains east of the Mispec River, where the valleys of the Caledonia Highlands were deep and narrow and did not fill with debris when the ice receded some ten thousand years before. This resulted in estuaries that reached back a long way toward the mountains from the Bay of Fundy. They formed a wide expanse of tidal flats at the river mouth rather than a dramatic drop to the bay as at Lepreau Falls in the west.

Much has changed in the landscape since Ganong's field trips, and a network of forest roads now makes a visit to the Mahood Lakes relatively easy. During my visit in the summer of 2012, I walked the ridge separating Adelaide and Ormond Lakes, looking without success for any evidence of the old military road Ganong alluded to in his report to the Natural History Society. The sandy beach he noted on Victoria Lake extends well out into the shallow lake and is unfortunately damaged by ATVs and four-wheel-drive trucks.

However, I discovered one strange anomaly in Ganong's report to the Natural History Society on the Lepreau field trip. Inexplicably, he overstated the height of both Ragged Falls and Big Falls, saying they were each over twenty-four metres (eighty feet) high, yet Ragged Falls is roughly a tenth of that height. There is no evidence that hydraulic action over the last century has changed the Lepreau River radically, nor do the surrounding topographical features support such a change. This is one of the rare occasions where Ganong either wanted to impress others with the wildness of the river, or he made a completely uncharacteristic mistake.

The Tobique Lass scow on the Tobique River, 1897

(NBM, William Francis Ganong Collection, Image 1987-17-1218-26)

5

The Complicated River

Nepisiguit Watershed, Summer 1899

The Nepisiguit, then, I submit, is a composite of four rivers, a small portion from the Tobique system, a very large part from the Upsalquitch system, a part from the Miramichi system, while the lower portion is the true Nepisiguit, which has worked back at its head, gradually capturing and making tributary to itself the aforementioned parts of the other systems.

— W.F. GANONG[1]

In the final years of the nineteenth century, Ganong carried out two extensive field trips into the heart of New Brunswick's wilderness. The first, in 1898, started in the Nepisiguit watershed and ended in the Tobique. The following summer, he began in the Tobique watershed and concluded in the Nepisiguit. From these two field trips, he learned to launch future field trips into the province's central highlands from the Tobique River to take advantage of the ease of travel to the upper reaches of the river and their access to the headwaters of several other important watersheds.

In 1899, after spending time at his summer home in Saint John, he travelled by train to Fredericton and then on to Newburg Junction near Woodstock. There he met his companion Mauran Furbish, a friend and fellow naturalist from Massachusetts. Throughout the trip, the two worked together to document the physiographic character of the river. Furbish's camera provided images of the trip, and Ganong scribbled field notes and sketched maps. Their data were later used in reports and also formed the basis for subsequent field trips, since the knowledge gained on each trip became the foundation for the next.

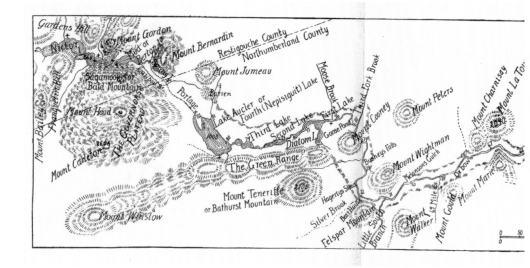

W.F. Ganong's map of Nictor [Nictau] Lake and the Upper Nepisiguit River (PANB-MC1799)

Eager to begin their fieldwork, the two men immediately journeyed by train farther up the Saint John River Valley to Perth-Andover, all the while noting the physiographic nature of the river. At Perth-Andover, they boarded another train for the trip to Plaster Rock where they hired horse and wagon to transport them up the Tobique River to either the settlement of Riley Brook or nearby Nictau.[2] With the tote road going only part way, they loaded their belongings onto a barge that was towed upriver by a team of oxen. It took two days to complete the forty-eight kilometre stretch, giving Ganong ample time to become acquainted with the Tobique Valley's physiography.

The settlements at Riley Brook and Nictau each had a hotel, frequented primarily by American sports during hunting and fishing trips.[3] Ganong often chose one of these communities as a starting point for his field trips, and occasionally as a place to rest before or after a particularly tiring journey. On this trip, the two explorers stayed only long enough to acquire a canoe, rations for the field trip, and the aid of a guide for the two-day trip up the Little Tobique River to Nictau (Nictor) Lake at the base of Mount Sagamook.

Ganong examined the lake and mountains thoroughly in order to understand the geology and record the physical geography of the area in detail. He surmised that Nictau Lake was formed by debris left behind after the last glaciers receded, also turning the waters of Lake Nepisiguit

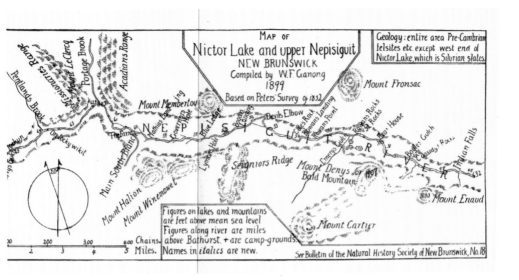

away from the Tobique River and towards the east and the Nepisiguit River. It was a theory that became the basis for much of his work on the formation of the province's river systems, a topic that he returned to over and over again.

> *In the whole of the attractive science of physiography, there is no subject of greater importance or interest than the changes, which river valleys undergo in the course of their evolution. Rivers are forever extending their basins and moving their watersheds, while frequently they capture other rivers. Hence it comes about that some rivers are composites of two or more streams originally separate.*[4]

The Nepisiguit River's constant changes in direction intrigued Ganong, who noted:

> *Twice in its course it bends permanently at right angles; it has a remarkably irregular drainage basin, and a valley which, through most of its extent, lessens in breadth and increases in slope towards its mouth. Such a river must have a complicated history, and it is, I believe a composite of four different river-systems.*[5]

Big Nictau Lake from Mount Sagamook, September 2014 and summer 1899

(Bottom: NBM, William Francis Ganong Collection, Image 1987-17-1218-228)

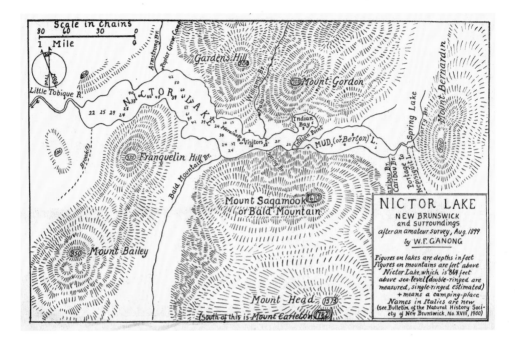

W.F. Ganong's map of Nictor (Nictau) Lake, 1899 (PANB-MC1799)

While at the lakes, Ganong and Furbish spent several days measuring the depth and the temperature of the water. The beauty and isolation of the lake impressed them deeply, and Ganong's report emphasizes its wilderness appeal:

> *At the eastern head of the Tobique River, in the north of the New Brunswick Highlands, lies Nictor, fairest of New Brunswick lakes. It is absolutely wild, unvisited save by an occasional sportsman or naturalist, and may be reached only by several-days canoe journey. It is un-surveyed, wrongly mapped, and scientifically little known.*[6]

As Ganong gathered data to map the lake correctly for the first time, he had for reference only the rudimentary historical maps then available. He noted of his equipment: "I used a fair prismatic compass, and a simple home-made apparatus on the stade principle for measuring distances; the general shape must be nearly accurate, though its proportions may be somewhat in error."[7] Despite any misgivings, he was later able to make detailed maps of the lake and river, ensuring that all essential features

Looking northwest across the Nepisiguit Lakes toward Governor's Plateau,
June 2012 and 1899 (Bottom: NBM, William Francis Ganong Collection, Image 1987-17-1218-45)

were noted. With Furbish's photographs, they provided the first accurate documentation of the lake and region.

Ganong and Furbish next ascended the difficult eastern face of Mount Sagamook. They determined that it was not a solitary peak but the northern point of a mountain chain that Ganong called the Governor's Plateau. A shallow valley separated Mount Sagamook from Mount Head and, farther to the south, Mount Carleton. Ganong wanted to determine if Sagamook was truly the highest peak in the province, rather than Big Bald Mountain at the headwaters of the South Branch Nepisiguit River. Although his measurements showed it was not, Sagamook won Ganong's heartfelt praise:

> *Above all and over all, however, towers grand Sagamook. Rising steeply over sixteen hundred feet directly from the lake, higher than any other New Brunswick hill rises from the water, clothed with living forest except for a few bold bosses near its summit, shrouded often in mists, it is easily the finest, even though not the highest, of New Brunswick hills.*[8]

Ganong still suspected that Big Bald might not be New Brunswick's highest peak, so he devised a plan to check it against Mount Carleton through "a comparison of careful theodolite measurements made from the summit of each."[9] With his characteristic determination, Ganong revisited the region in 1903 and conducted aneroid barometric measurements for greater accuracy, determining that the mountain he named Mount Carleton was actually the highest in the province.

Exploration of the mountains and lake finished, Ganong and Furbish left the region by portaging from Nictau Lake over the height of land to Bathurst Lake and the Nepisiguit Lakes at the head of the Nepisiguit River. They followed a route that had been a traditional Mi'kmaq portage between the watersheds. Before canoeing down the river, the two men explored the lakes. In a small inlet near Mount Teneriffe, they took temperature and depth readings from a shallow area where the bottom lay only inches from the surface. Ganong also sampled the content and consistency of the mud and concluded that, like many of the mud lakes in the province, the inlet had been formed by the continuous deposit of decayed organic material that he later determined to be alive with algae and diatomic plants.

Below the lake system, the river twisted and turned through a magnificent chain of mountains to its confluence with Silver Brook. The scientists stopped frequently to take side trips to the tops of mountains and up the river's major tributaries. They measured distances and elevations, determined physiographical features, and gathered information for future fieldwork. These side trips also fulfilled the secondary role of determining the likely paths of the many Native portage routes.

From previous field trips, Ganong expected to find a portage between the Nepisiguit watershed and the Upsalquitch River, but he was unsure of its exact location. Just below Silver Brook, the river straightened and opened into a wide valley. They set up camp at the mouth of the promisingly named Portage Brook. Ganong suspected that the valley might once have been a river that flowed north into the Upsalquitch, making it a logical portage route. He was close but not close enough. "After much debate as to whether to go by canoe or risk the portage now," he recorded in his field notes, "— decided for latter — and travelled 8 miles up Portage without of course reaching the lake and returned disgusted."[10] When Ganong returned in 1903, he discovered just how close he had been, noting: "there is a low and easy portage to Upsalquitch Lake, which lies 100 feet lower than the mouth of Portage Brook."[11]

Ganong and Furbish continued paddling downriver, stopping at the confluence of the Nepisiguit with the South Branch to reconnoitre before Indian Falls, a series of rapids that stretched almost a kilometre. They camped at the lower end of the falls, adjacent to a deep pool where trout and salmon were plentiful. An enthusiastic Furbish wrote in his diary: "Ran to Indian Falls and portaged before dinner — enjoyed delightful afternoon fishing, loafing — the finest day of the trip."[12]

The paddling to this point was smooth and brisk, but Ganong found the river beyond the falls to be geologically different, reporting:

> *This part of the river, from Indian Falls to Nepisiguit Brook, is very puzzling, and I have not been able to form any clear idea of its probable mode of formation. . . . Certainly all this part of the main Nepisiguit must be comparatively new, much newer than the upper section of the river.*[13]

Mount Teneriffe from the Nepisiguit Lakes, June 2012 and 1899

(Bottom: NBM, William Francis Ganong Collection, Image 1987-17-1218-3)

The Upper Nepisiguit River, June 2012 and 1899

(Bottom: NBM, William Francis Ganong Collection, Image 1987-17-1218-2)

Beginning at Nepisiguit Brook, ledges and the narrowing river created many cataracts, meaning tricky paddling and more portages. Ganong hypothesized that the section between the falls and the narrows was a part of the Northwest Miramichi River that glacial action had rerouted. Along the north bank of the river just above the narrows, he spent a day inspecting large flat stones that appeared to have been fitted together. He attributed the phenomenon to large amounts of glacial meltwater that coursed through the narrows and forced boulders into the softer soil, smoothing their upwards-facing portions to create a surface resembling a cobblestone road.

Below the narrows was a magnificent Nepisiguit Falls,[14] and a sheer walled gorge rose high above the narrow channel. It ended in what British and American sports considered one of the finest salmon pools in the province. Although the river valley gradually widened after the pool, some narrow channels with challenging rapids and cascades occurred, notably at Middle Landing.[15] The river finally became easier paddling below Pabineau Falls, Boucher Falls, and the stretch known as Rough Water. Ganong and Furbish soon approached the Bay of Chaleur and the town of Bathurst and the end of their expedition.

Through this field trip, Ganong became concerned that the cutting of trees along the Nepisiguit, Tobique, and Miramichi watersheds threatened to forever scar the Nictau Lake wilderness. In an 1899 presentation titled "The Forestry Problem In New Brunswick," he called the unmanaged forest the province's greatest natural wealth and warned that it was deteriorating steadily. He felt that the general public of the time was uninformed and thus indifferent and that the government was not taking an active role in proper resource management. He condemned short-sighted forestry practices, writing:

> *No pulp mill should be allowed to operate in New Brunswick in a way to deforest any piece of land, for a speedy profit of this kind will be dearly paid for in the future. The only wise method in forestry management is to keep a forest intact, and this can be done only by a system of rotation in cutting, by which the larger trees alone are removed, the smaller being left to grow.*[16]

The gorge below
the Nepisiguit Falls,
May 2008

Ganong's work to understand the Nepisiguit River formation was also instrumental in developing his system of classification for New Brunswick rivers. In the spring of 1899, he presented a paper, "On a Division of New Brunswick Into Physiographic Districts," to the Natural History Society. The divisions, based on river systems and geological irregularities, helped to explain the province's historic travel routes and the distribution of settlement and brought together human and natural history. Through Ganong's research, other members of the society also began to understand the importance of the region, especially the headwaters of the Nepisiguit and Tobique watersheds.

In the conclusion of another paper, "On The Physiography of the Nictor Lake Region,"[17] Ganong urged the citizens of New Brunswick to protect this valuable wilderness for future generations. "Nictor Lake, therefore, lies to-day not only by nature that most charming place in the interior of New Brunswick, but as yet entirely unspoiled," he argued, going on to ask: "But why should not the people of New Brunswick prevent its despoiling, and set aside the lake and its shores as a provincial park, to be kept wild and beautiful for their enjoyment forever."[18]

6

A Sportsman's Paradise
The Negoot (Tobique) Lakes, Summer 1900

There is no name in use for this group of lakes as a whole, and
hence I have ventured to apply to them the ancient Maliseet
name of the Tobique River, that is Negoot.... It's [*sic*] meaning
is unknown, but I suspect it is connected with Nik-taak, Forks,
in reference to the repeated forking of the Right Hand Branch.

— W.F. GANONG[1]

With the beginning of a new century, Ganong's resolve to document the
physiographic nature of New Brunswick intensified. His field trips were
increasingly well planned, with specific objectives and desired outcomes
based on information gathered on previous trips. As the trips became
more extensive, they required a stamina and determination that took a
toll on his companions, both physically and emotionally. In the summer
of 1900, Ganong once again used the Tobique River as a staging area,
this time to travel into the headwaters he named the Negoot lakes. His
friends George Upham Hay and Mauran Furbish accompanied him on
the three-week expedition.

One reason for this trip was to determine the relationship between the
Tobique and Little Southwest Miramichi watersheds. Ganong had sketched
the outline of these lakes and the surrounding hills when he climbed
Mount Carleton in 1899. Then over the winter, he gathered information
from geological surveys and members of the Natural History Society to
gain a historical perspective. An unhurried journey upriver provided
opportunities to discuss its physiographic attributes with his companions.
They noted that the main Tobique runs southwest, parallel to two distinct

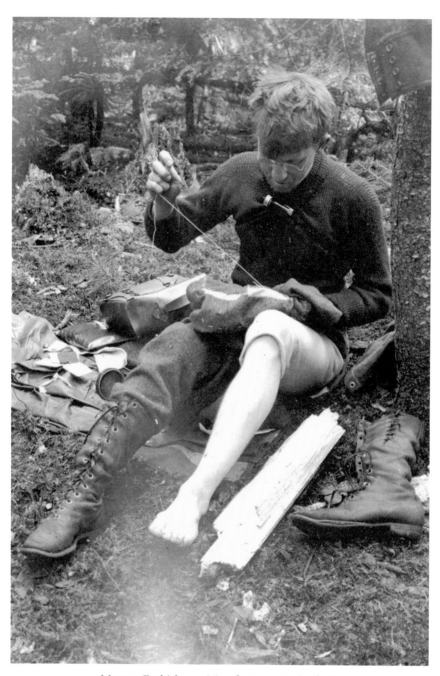

Mauran Furbish repairing footwear in the field

(NBM, William Francis Ganong Collection, Image 1987-17-1218-150)

The majestic Tobique River, Victoria County, August 2014

series of hills rising more than five hundred feet. Ganong surmised that it was relatively unchanged since postglacial times and "despite its apparent complexity, appears to be a comparatively simple river with a steady and homogenous development."[2]

At a stop in Plaster Rock to retrieve a cache of dry goods, Ganong investigated the red sandstone escarpment along the river and inquired about unusual local phenomena such as the reputed warm patch on nearby Blue Mountain, said to remain free of snow all winter. Stopping again in Nictau, Ganong took stock of their supplies and scientific equipment before heading south on the Trowsers (Trousers) Lake portage road to the Negoot or South Tobique Lakes.

It was a wilderness region of unnamed lakes and streams. As a way of acknowledging his friend's contribution to the research, Ganong named one pond at the head of the watershed Furbish Pond and another Mauran Lake. He noted that the lakes lay within a peneplain that formed the central highlands of New Brunswick.[3] Ganong was certain that all of the lakes that make up the Negoot were formed by glacial drift damming ancient rivers within the series of parallel valleys. His research revealed that these valleys extended to one elevated ridge that separated them from the Miramichi River. Ganong hiked to the height of land though he did not find the natural portage to the head of the Little Southwest Miramichi

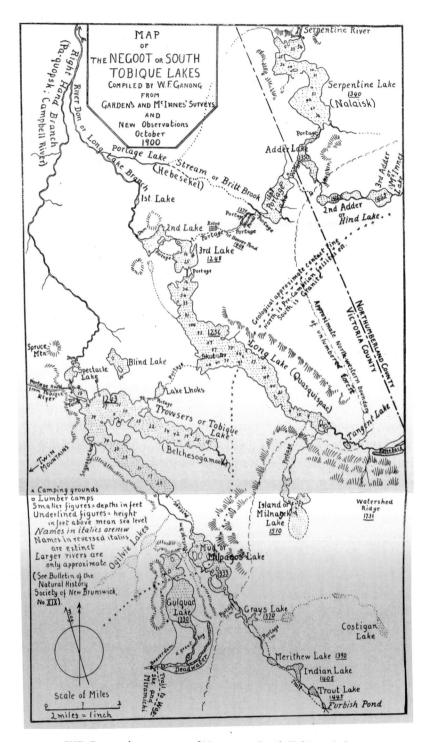

W.F. Ganong's 1900 map of Negoot or South Tobique Lakes

(PANB-MC1799)

River via Long Lake until a subsequent trip. However, he did find that there were well-worn trails connecting lakes and streams throughout the region, indicating long-term use by First Nations hunters as well as guides and their sports.

The men then canoed the west branch of Trowsers Lake, paddling through a chain of lakes and finally into the shallows of a cove at the southernmost reaches of the watershed. Ganong carefully mapped the land separating the right branch of the Tobique River from the headwaters of the Renous River. He recorded that the well-forested mountaintops were unlike the rocky peaks found along the Nepisiguit River and would be a sportsman's paradise.

> *Everywhere one is impressed by the innumerable smoothly-rounded hills and ridges of moderate height, by the splendid living forest which completely covers them, by the number and beauty of the lakes, by the swiftness of the streams, by the abundance of big animals, moose, caribou, deer and beaver, by all-pervading remoteness, wilderness and primitiveness.*[4]

As with previous field trips, Ganong measured the elevations of the hills and lakes, while noting their physiographic attributes and mapping their locations. For accuracy, he measured the elevation of the surface of Trowsers Lake fifteen times. Furbish took the same measurements independently, and his numbers were, for the most part, in agreement with Ganong's. During this and subsequent field trips, Ganong compared other lakes and ponds to the Trowsers Lake findings. The lake had been dammed to provide driving power for log drives down the Tobique River. As he reported to the Natural History Society, this affected both the condition of the lake and the accuracy of some measurements. "Trowsers Lake is attractive, though injured by the dead trees killed by the dam at its outlet," he wrote. "This dam holds the water some six feet above the normal level, so that for natural depth the figures on the map are six feet too high."[5]

Heading east overland, Ganong, Hay, and Furbish reached Long Lake, where Ganong again conducted a series of measurements. At 35.7 metres (117 feet), Long Lake was the deepest measured during his field trips to this point. He later learned of a deeper one in Madawaska County and noted the work of Joseph Bailey, the son of Loring Woart Bailey. "Mr. J.W.

Ganong surveying Long Lake, Negoot (Tobique) Lakes, 1901

(NBM, William Francis Ganong Collection, Image 1987-17-1218-129)

Bailey tells me, however, that he has obtained 165 feet in Glazier Lake, on the St. Francis, near the New Brunswick side."[6]

Of all the lakes in the region, Ganong found Long Lake to be the most appealing. He was particularly impressed by the hills that separated the lake from the Miramichi watershed where he and his two companions hiked southeast to the location of a remarkable spring that flows into the Little Southwest Miramichi. About six-and-a-half kilometres from the edge of Long Lake, they located a strange clear pool of water "nearly circular, and some two or three feet across and over a foot deep, and is especially peculiar in this, that its water surface stands a foot or more above the general level of the ground, held up to that height by a symmetrical wall forming a regular basin, as a lake may be held in the crater of a volcano."[7]

From Long Lake, they carried their canoe and supplies to Portage Lake and then into the headwaters of one of the Tobique's large tributaries, the Serpentine River. As its name implies, the Serpentine River snakes through the high mountains that form the southern boundary of the Tobique Valley. Ganong climbed Mount Nalaisk and the Serpentine Mountain, two of the area's most striking features, to measure their heights and to take compass readings to both Mount Carleton in the east and Bald Peak to the southwest. With evident excitement he reported: "As one descends the Serpentine River from the lake, he sees, as he nears the Stillwater, a splendid double mountain towering before him, which impresses him as not only the highest on the river, but as one of the highest in the province." [8]

Ganong and his companions made their way back to the settlement of Riley Brook for a short rest and then hiked into the highlands to Bald Head (Bald Peak):

> Bald Head, in many respects is the most striking, easily-recognized and mountain-like mountain in New Brunswick. It rises perfectly abruptly some thousand feet above a flat basin, and its steep bare top is a conspicuous and unmistakable object from every direction. It is locally reputed to be simply a heap of loose stones, which well describes the impression it makes upon one, but the description is not correct, for the top is of ledge rock.[9]

Ganong noted that the southern slope was ledge rock and the northern an elongated boulder field, unusual for a mountain of this sort since the northern face, against the direction of the glacial ice-shield, normally would be abrupt. As botanist, Ganong and Hay found several small sphagnum bogs on the northern slope, which required a steady supply of fresh water that seemed perplexing at that elevation. As he reported to the society:

The other explanation is that there is some peculiarity in the structure of this mountain which produces the storage of water under the rocks in spots, allowing it to escape gradually after the manner of springs. But no trace of such a structure is to be seen. The subject is very puzzling.[10]

This side trip to the mountain completed Ganong's field trip to the region. He documented the terrain throughout the region, detailing the

Bald (Head) Peak, Victoria County, September 2012 and 1900

(Bottom: NBM, William Francis Ganong Collection, Image 1987-17-1218-80)

relationship between the Negoot chain of lakes and the Tobique and Miramichi Rivers. With this information, he began to piece together the physiographic characteristics of the region for his many reports on the summer's fieldwork.

When I visited the area for two days in September 2012, both Trousers and Long Lakes were at least three metres shallower than normal. Currently, these lakes are part of the water containment for the NB Power hydro dam at the Tobique Narrows. Unlike the wilderness experienced by Ganong, I found numerous logging roads criss-crossing the entire region and an active forestry operation. Yet it remains a beautiful area with lush meadows tucked into rolling hillsides and abundant wildlife. On my trip, I encountered moose, deer, rabbit, partridge, and beaver. On a turn in the road, I was fortunate to glimpse a bobcat before it hightailed into the woods, and while I was eating lunch, a coyote sauntered toward my truck and then veered off into the forest. Today, as in the late 1800s and early 1900s, the Tobique Lakes region is a sportsman's paradise.

Late afternoon on the Crooked Deadwater, October 2012

7

The Primeval Wilderness

The Little Southwest Miramichi River, Summer 1901

I crossed New Brunswick from the Tobique River to the
mouth of the Miramichi, by way of Trowsers, Long, Milnagek
(Island), Little Southwest (Tuadook) Lakes and the Little
Southwest Miramichi River.

— W.F. GANONG[1]

Never wanting to leave fieldwork incomplete, Ganong returned to the
Negoot Lakes in the summer of 1901 to undertake an ambitious field trip
and to conclude unfinished research. His focus that summer was the relationship between the Negoot branch of the Tobique watershed and the
Little Southwest Miramichi watershed. Ganong's need to collect accurate
data led him to undertake an extended elevation study from the Tobique
to the Little Southwest Miramichi. To ensure accuracy, he used three
different instruments, which he personally calibrated. Prior to the trip
he took baseline measurements at Fredericton and Chatham to provide
an accurate comparison for all future elevation measurements, writing in
his report: "The instruments and methods used, and the care exercised in
all observations and calculations are such as to make me feel confident."[2]

After spending time in Riley Brook to rest and gather supplies, he and
Mauran Furbish retraced their trip of the previous summer along the portage road to the Negoot Lakes. Gaining confidence with their wilderness
skills, they went without a guide on this trip, preferring to go it alone.
This was not out of character for Ganong, who often preferred solitude
during his trips. At Trowsers Lake they spent a few days re-measuring
elevations and checking for consistent results. On August 3, 1901, while

camping on the shore, they witnessed the uncommon sight of a lunar rainbow over the lake.

> *About ten o'clock, a light shower with fleecy clouds came up opposite to the waning but bright moon, and against the clouds appeared a very perfect bow with the arch complete. No colors were visible, but instead the bow was a grayish light, not unlike the northern streamers.*[3]

Ganong and Furbish departed Trowsers Lake, pushing farther inland by way of an old portage trail to gain access to Long Lake. Retracing the route used in 1900, they paddled down its length, all the while taking elevation measurements, to the mouth of a small brook emptying from Milnagek Lake. A high ridge forming the southern end of Long Lake meant they had to carry their equipment and line their canoe up the turbulent brook as they explored for the shortest path from the Right Hand Branch Tobique watershed, to the Little Southwest Miramichi. From Milnagek, the companions made their way to Squaw Lake and the surrounding Squaw Barren in the Central Highlands before returning to spend several more days recording data on the lake and the surrounding hills that form the divide between the watersheds. He noted of Squaw Barren:

> *On the west it drains into Squaw Lake, an affluent of Tobique, and on the southwest into Rumsey Lake, a beaver pond draining into the Little Southwest Miramichi. It cannot often be that a bog forms the watershed between two systems so important.*[4]

Ganong considered the high lake and its feeder ponds to be among the most scenic areas in the province:

> *The scenery of Milnagek is beautiful. On the east, south and west the hills rise 200 to 300 feet near the lake, and are densely wooded with a fine, mixed forest, above which towers often the stately pine. The lake is studded with islands, all heavily forested, and between them and into the coves are many most charming vistas.*[5]

The Little Southwest Miramichi rises in the ancient central highlands of New Brunswick. From these ridges, several small tributaries drop quickly

The outlet of Pocket Lake, July 2011; 1901

(Right: NBM, William Francis Ganong Collection, Image 1987-17-1218-148)

into a wide, heavily wooded basin, where they meander through barrens and wetlands, forming lakes and long deadwaters. Ganong and Furbish eventually made their way down from the highlands and through the Crooked Deadwater, around Braithwaite Mountain to Pocket Lake. The outlet of this small lake was a rock-strewn brook, like many in the region, of boulder and bog, which made it challenging to reach Tuadook Lake in the Miramichi watershed.

Ganong considered Tuadook, the largest of the Southwest Miramichi Lakes and speckled with islands, most picturesque. The pair of explorers spent several days at Henry Braithwaite's camp on the lake, noting the physiographical attributes of the lakes — the low plateau and the ridges — as well as the richness and diversity of the surrounding forest. Braithwaite was one of New Brunswick's foremost guides and woodsmen of the 1800s and owned hunting camps from the Southwest Miramichi River across to Upsalquitch Lake.[6] Ganong greatly admired his knowledge of the area.

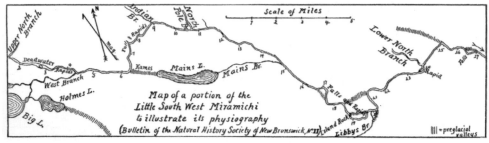

W.F. Ganong's 1901 map of a portion of the Little South West Miramichi
(PANB-MC1799)

*This entire region is notable as the hunting and trapping ground
of that prince of hunters, Mr. Henry Braithwaite, who knows it
intimately, and who takes to it a number of sportsmen each autumn.
It is a pity that Mr. Braithwaite's knowledge of its topography and
natural history cannot, through publication, be made available to
others and safe from loss.[7]*

Leaving the camp at Tuadook Lake, Furbish and Ganong were forced to pull
their canoe and supplies down the boulder-strewn Tuadook River to join
the Little Southwest Miramichi at Smith Forks. From the forks the river
was navigable, but this changed abruptly where it turned to the northeast.

Beyond the six-and-one-half mile turn (measured from the forks with
the West Branch Little Southwest), the river knifed through high ridges,
forming falls and rapids and forcing Ganong and Furbish to land and
portage through this rugged section along a pathway used by lumbermen
and conceivably First Nations people. Ganong noted the river's increasing
roughness:

*At the six and one half mile turn the river bends abruptly north-
ward.... Less than a mile below this turn, at an elevation of 1045
feet or less, begin the bad rapids and falls which have made this
river famous. Here the river narrows and falls over granite ledges
and through small gorges with vertical granite walls.[8]*

Ganong found the change puzzling until he determined that the origin
was a series of kames or low sand hills that were deposited by a retreating
glacier. He tracked the ancient riverbed over a series of these hills to Mains

Lake and followed Mains Brook as it led back to the Little Southwest. Ganong concluded that the glacier had redirected the river, later reporting:

> *The interpretation of these facts might be difficult enough were it not for another brought out by the maps, namely, that in a line between the six and one-half mile bend and the mouth of Mains Brook lies the valley occupied by Mains Lake and Brook. All these facts taken together seem to point to but one conclusion, namely that in preglacial times the main river flowed through the present valley of Mains Lake and Brook. The kame hills at the six and one half mile bend constitute the great glacial dam which turned the river aside and sent it over a low part of its valley.*[9]

The river's difficult temperament persisted to Indian Brook and North Pole Stream, where Ganong noted that the river was less tumultuous and remained so until what he identified as the "17-mile turn," where the original riverbed had again been dammed with glacial debris and the relatively new channel cut through a narrow, V-shaped valley with ridges high above.

From here to the mouth of Libbies Brook is the wildest section of the river. Ganong noted that the river dropped ten metres (thirty-two feet) per mile from the fork with the West Branch, where they entered the main river, to Libbies Brook, a distance of twenty-four kilometres, or fifteen miles.

At Libbies Brook they hiked a short distance to see a postglacial waterfall and an exposed ancient peneplain, characteristic of the surrounding valley. From the brook to the confluence of the Lower North Branch, the Little Southwest Miramichi River continued to drop steadily, with only a few rapids. Ganong noted that the character of the river and surrounding valley changed again below Catamaran Brook where the topology began to slope gently away from the river, producing terraces of fine sand and, further on, a broad valley. In this lower section, the river meandered around low islands before meeting the Northwest Miramichi at Red Bank. The field trip finished downriver in Newcastle, and Ganong returned to Saint John, then travelled to Massachusetts for another winter of writing and planning for the following summer.

Gary Tozer accompanied me on my trip to photograph Flaherty's Pitch. We hiked down to Libbies Falls and then upriver along the Little Southwest to Flaherty's on a footpath located on a ridge above the river. It is a most spectacular section of the river. We then backtracked and drove

Libbies Falls on the Little Southwest Miramichi River,
May 2009 and 1901. Note the rolling dam commonly
used to allow timber logs to shoot over waterfalls
and Ganong examining the exposed peneplain.

(Bottom: NBM, William Francis Ganong Collection, Image 1987-17-1218-166)

out and parked on a logging road near an area called Loggies Lodge for a short hike through the woods to Indian Falls.

Later that summer we drove out to Tuadook Lake. This required a drive on a very rock-strewn road and then a hike to the lake around large boulders. While at the lake we hiked to the stream that connects Pocket Lake with Tuadook.

In early October of the same year, I decided to make a solo trip out to the Crooked Deadwater. I prepared for an overnight stay to catch the waning light of day. Fortunately I chose an unseasonably warm night to camp in the woods. The drive out from the Renous highway was a bit tenuous, as my GPS and maps did not agree on the route I chose from my reconnaissance of Google Earth. Eventually, the GPS began to chirp, indicating my desired destination. The effort was well worth the image I shot that afternoon.

Looking west towards Adder Lake Stream, October 2012

8

Uncharted Country

Central Highlands and Upsalquitch River, Summer 1902

The region is but rarely visited, is for the most part not yet
opened up by guides for sporting purposes, and needless to say,
has not yet been visited by any geologist or other naturalist.

— W.F. GANONG[1]

In the summer of 1902, Ganong once again returned to the headwaters of
the Tobique with Mauran Furbish. This time, their plan was to spend two
weeks mapping an area he called Adder Lake Stream Basin. This section of
the Tobique River — and the province, for that matter — was unfamiliar
and uncharted, which was more than enough to bring Ganong back to the
Tobique watershed. He was most interested in a section of the highlands
region called Upper Grahams Plain.

He and Furbish hiked through an open area dotted with boulders and
clusters of stunted shrubs, noting:

> *The most striking part of the region is the Upper Graham Plains,
> a remarkable open elevated barren, covered with boulders, among
> which are some low scrubby heath bushes, lichens and the occasional
> whitened trunks of former small trees.*[2]

Turning over some lichen, he found the charred remains of trees. Past forest
fires had ravaged the barren, exposing numerous boulders and rocky soil.
He decided that "this plain is misnamed for it is by no means a plain, but
an irregular country with a general slope to the northward; indeed it is
chiefly the gentle northern slope of a mountain some 1900 feet in height."[3]

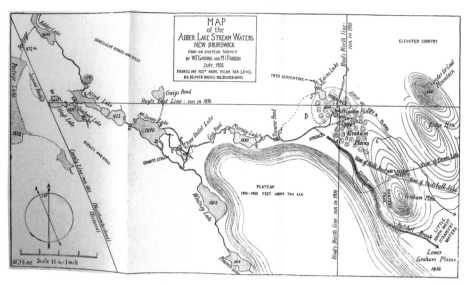

W.F. Ganong's map of Adder Lake Stream (PANB-MC1799)

Ganong found numerous game trails through the basin, and he strongly suggested that it be set aside as a game refuge and breeding ground for the larger animals, such as caribou and moose. From the elevated plain he could see in all directions, providing an opportunity to map the entire region and to determine its physiographic characteristics.

Ganong wanted to explore Patchell Brook, located in the transition between Upper and Lower Graham Plains. The formation of this brook and its ravine intrigued him. An absence of forest made a tiny rivulet clearly visible "amidst great angular blocks of felsite at the bottom of an immense V-shaped gorge with solid felsite walls some 300 to 400 feet in height."[4] Later, he commented that the scene was more like one in the Rocky Mountains than in New Brunswick. Ganong wondered how such a small brook could carve such a deep ravine into the granite hillside. After much consideration he speculated that the ravine was a fault line running in a southeast direction. Meltwater from the receding glacier together with water from the Serpentine River and Adder Lake that had been blocked by glacial debris had channelled into the fault. This enormous amount of water, rock, and rubble carved the gorge and deposited the boulders at the base of the ridge. Ganong outlined the process in his November 1902 address to the Natural History Society:

These combined influences would tend to send a great quantity of water loaded with glacial debris, out through Patchell Brook, and this I believe, cut out the gorge in the comparatively short period during the melting of the glacial ice in this vicinity. The debris carried down the gorge was then spread out where it issued on the lower plain, forming the Lower Graham Plain, which is thus a rude delta of that stream.[5]

With their exploration of the plains finished, Ganong and Furbish returned to Nictau for a short rest and to hire a canoe and purchase additional supplies. Ganong wanted to complete research that he'd begun in 1899 in the headwaters of the Upsalquitch River. The two men began by poling the canoe up the Little Tobique River to Lake Nictor (Nictau). Next they carried their gear over the short portage to Lake Nepisiguit and canoed down the Nepisiguit River to Portage Brook. Poling up the brook, they located the long-established portage route between the Nepisiguit and Restigouche Rivers at the mouth of Meadow Brook. At Meadow Brook they canoed up looking for a location that best suited a starting point of the overland portion of the portage. Then they hauled their canoe, scientific gear, and supplies on an exhausting portage over the height of land to Upsalquitch Lake and into the Restigouche watershed.

Ganong's 1904 report to the Natural History Society makes it apparent that he was taken by the pristine nature of Upsalquitch Lake and the surrounding mountains. He and Furbish stayed for several days, mapping the lake, sketching and measuring the height of mountains, and piecing together an idea of the preglacial physiography. Ganong speculated that the valley had tilted slightly postglacially, forcing Meadow Brook to turn away from its original course and flow into Portage Brook and the Nepisiguit. He noted: "I am inclined to think these upper Nepisiguit waters must have flowed into the Upsalquitch up to the glacial period, and that it was some form of glacial action which produced the change."[6]

Ganong wrote that no fewer than ten noteworthy mountains, unnamed prior to his visit, surrounded Upsalquitch Lake. He named the entire mountain range the Naturalist Group, and gave each peak the name of a prominent person or scientist who, in his opinion, furthered the understanding of natural history. Furbish named the highest and most prominent peak Mount Ganong, in honour of his fellow explorer. The two

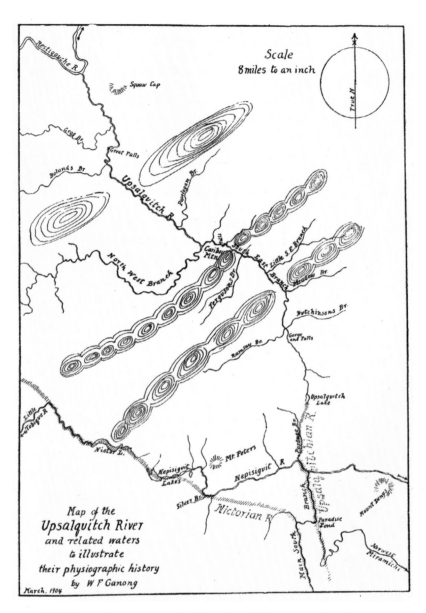

W.F. Ganong's 1904 map of the Upsalquitch River and related waters

(PANB-MC1799)

Looking towards the outlet of Upsalquitch Lake and the Naturalist Mountains, July 1902 (NBM, William Francis Ganong Collection Image 1987-17-1218-11)

men climbed to the summit of each mountain to survey and document the salient features of the watershed.

As with other wilderness locations that he had documented, Ganong felt that the basin between the Upsalquitch and Nepisiguit watersheds should be set aside as a nature preserve for further study. He was particularly concerned about this watershed's First Nations' portage route because it was still intact, not yet altered by logging or roads. He noted, though, that lumbering was threatening even this remote, pristine area:

> It is a coincidence more curious than gratifying that the lumbermen have reached Nictor, Nepisiguit and Upsalquitch Lakes almost simultaneously. Lumbering on the two former was just commenced last winter (1901-1902) and is to be prosecuted actively the present winter (1902-1903), as it is to be on Upsalquitch Lake.[7]

Ganong and Furbish next pushed north through the meadows of the Southeast Upsalquitch River. Ganong knew that sportsmen had previously followed this branch of the river, but there was scant written information. Ganong had found a published journal recording Captain Richard Lewes Dashwood's hunting trip to the area in 1863, entitled Chiploquorgan. Maps

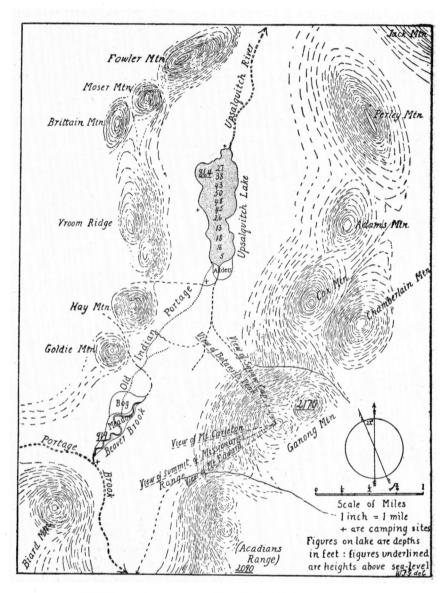

W.F. Ganong's 1902 map of Upsalquitch Lake (PANB-MC1799)

of the lake and the upper reaches of the river lacked essential details, though Ganong's map borrowed much from the crude sketches of the mouth of the river that the cartographer Joseph Frederick DesBarres drew in 1780.[8] Ganong also relied on the county line survey map of 1872.

After pushing and pulling their canoe through sluggish water shrouded in heavy brush, they reached the confluence with Eighteen-Mile Brook. Here the Upsalquitch became rougher as it flowed over a series of ledges before the beginning of the Southeast Gorge. There, the river changed dramatically again as "eight miles from the lake, it plunges into a typical, post glacial gorge two miles in length, in which the water, by a series of falls and rocky rapids, drops some 150 feet."[9] Ganong remarked on the breathtaking ruggedness of the gorge, with sheer cliffs and lush forest creating a beautiful natural setting.

The men portaged around the gorge and camped on a flat strip of land used by aboriginal peoples for centuries. Not one to ignore an opportunity, Ganong searched the portage and campsite for artifacts and ascended the gorge to examine its geological characteristics. Further down the Southeast Branch he climbed Caribou Mountain and found that it was one in a series of mountains running east and west. He took elevation measurements, made notes on the geology and studied the physiography of the lower watershed. Familiar with the geological maps of the time, he recommended an adjustment based on his findings. Below the falls, the river emerged into a broad valley and met the calmer waters of the Northwest Branch at the Upsalquitch Forks:

> Below the Forks the Upsalquitch is a large and very charming river, of grand scenery, swift and abundant clear water affording ideal canoeing, extensive intervales, and all the beauties characteristic of the best of our New Brunswick Rivers. [10]

Ganong and Furbish finished the summer field trip at Atholville before beginning the long train journey back to Saint John. For Mauran Furbish, this gruelling summer of 1902 was his last field trip into the New Brunswick wilderness with Ganong.

On a hot, humid August morning in 2011, Gary Tozer and I drove into a large clear-cut in Lower Grahams Plain with plans to photograph the Patchell Brook ravine that Ganong had compared to the Rockies. Looking at the mountains that surrounded our route, I began to appreciate the scope

Passing storm on Mount Ganong, June 2011

of the hike. After a morning scrambling through heavy brush and deadfalls amidst blackflies and smothering heat, I finally collapsed on a rock where my GPS indicated the brook should have been. I could hear the gurgle of water, but the trees, brush, and huge scattered boulders completely hid it from view. Our hike continued up to the ridge forming the southwest edge of the ravine, but after struggling for forty-five minutes to hike half a kilometre, we resigned ourselves to returning another time.

The following May, Rod O'Connell, Karl Branch, and I found a more direct route to the ravine. We started from a clear-cut located in the transition zone where the upper plain slopes to the southeast, dropping more than one hundred and fifty metres to Lower Graham Plain. Like the lower section, it is now scribed with logging roads and has undergone intensive harvesting. We made it to the ravine and revelled in this unique geological phenomenon. I suspect little has changed in the ravine itself, except for the clear-cuts that surround it. As I photographed the ravine, I thought about Ganong painstakingly mapping the gorge and pondering the reasons for its formation.

9

A Nomadic Life

North Branch Oromocto River, South Branch Nepisiguit
River, and Northwest Miramichi River, Summer 1903

The inconveniences of his nomadic life meant nothing to
him as long as information was forthcoming.

— SUSAN B. GANONG[1]

Ganong's itinerary for 1903 left little time for leisure. The summer started
with a July trip from Oromocto Lake down the North Branch Oromocto
River to its confluence with the South Branch and then further down to
the Saint John River. His second field trip was more extreme, taking him
back to the Nepisiguit River to explore the turbulent South Branch.

Friend and colleague George Upham Hay accompanied him on the
first trip to study the physiographic character and natural history of the
Oromocto Lake and the North Branch Oromocto River for the first time.
As well, much of the lower portion of the North Branch of the Oromocto
River valley had been surveyed as part of land grants, but Ganong wanted
to better map the upper reaches near the lake. They arrived at Oromocto
Lake by wagon from Saint John with their canoe and supplies. After establishing a campsite, Hay documented the area's flora, finding no new
species, and Ganong measured the lake's depth, temperature, and elevation
above sea level.

Ganong noted the historical use of the North Branch as a portage route
by First Nations, the French, and the Loyalists, resulting in quite detailed
maps. However, the maps had only an approximate portage location, and
locals were similarly uninformed about the trail. The North Branch was
the overland connection in a traditional canoe route from the Saint John

Dr. William Francis Ganong standing near Sucker Brook, Harvey Lake

(NBM, William Francis Ganong Collection, Image 1987-17-1218-240)

River to Passamaquoddy Bay and a reason why Ganong considered the Oromocto one of New Brunswick's most important rivers. The "old Indian portage path," as indicated on his map, "followed the low place in the ridge a little north of a direct line between the two ends."[2]

Ganong and Hay camped at White Sand Cove near the Oromocto end of the portage. As always, Ganong speculated on the area's geological history. He concluded from the elevated ridge separating Oromocto Lake and the Magaguadavic River, and from the orientation with smaller lakes to the southwest, that the lake had likely been part of the Magaguadavic watershed. Glacial events eons before had turned it towards the North Branch Oromocto River. Ganong inspected Kelly's Island closely, concluding it had probably been formed when the melting glacier shed an erratic. Based on rocky debris scattered throughout the valley, he deduced that the North Branch was postglacial in formation from the lake to the confluence with Yoho Stream.

Their survey of the area completed, the two men paddled away from the eastern side of the lake, canoeing easily along the quiet deadwaters through Barton Rips and past Lyon Stream. Ganong noted a set of falls and cliffs above Hartt's Island, and where a forest fire had exposed the

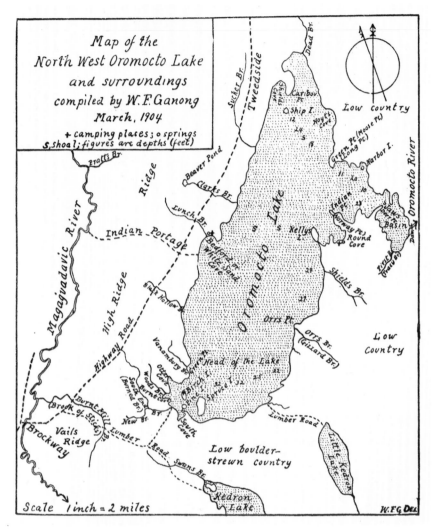

W.F. Ganong's 1903 map of Oromocto Lake (PANB-MC1799)

landscape at Otter Brook, he identified "two of the most perfect drumlins, one of them conical, that I have seen in New Brunswick."[3]

They camped at Yoho Stream where Ganong used his survey equipment and compass to determine the exact orientation of the ridge forming the south bank. He noted that the ridge crossed the North Branch Oromocto River, leaving a series of ledges just below its surface, and continued along the south bank. Based on the topology of this section of river, Ganong speculated that the North Branch originally had its headwaters at Yoho Lake or beyond and not Oromocto Lake.

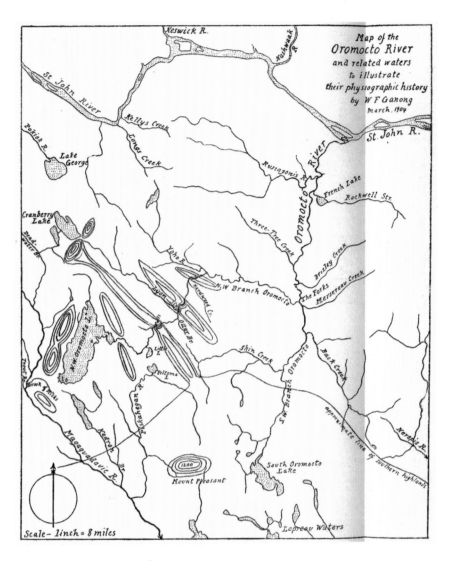

W.F. Ganong's 1904 map of Oromocto River (PANB-MC1799)

Continuing down the North Branch, they passed the settlements of Tracy and Fredericton Junction, where the river turned abruptly south and then east over the postglacial falls and rapids commonly known as both White's Rapids and Gaspereau Falls. Ganong noted that the preglacial valley would have been on the south side of the river, but he did not take time to map it.[4] Below the rapids, the river entered a marshy basin, slowing almost to a deadwater before meeting the more turbulent South Branch Oromocto River. In his 1904 report, Ganong stated:

This part of the river I have not visited and know nothing of.
Noting the direction of the lake (South Oromocto Lake), however,
its relation to Mahood's Lake, to the small lakes northwest of it
and to the head of Shin Creek, I think it is extremely probable that
all of these occupy one very ancient valley, which in former times
ran across the southern highlands, giving a continuous river from
Lepreau to Cranberry Lake by Lyons Stream.[5]

A tributary of the South Branch called Back Creek especially intrigued
Ganong. Its physiographic relationship with Douglas Valley Brook, a tributary of the Nerepis River that in turn led into the Saint John River, made
him suspect that Back Creek was the preglacial channel that connected
the Oromocto River with the Saint John River.

This raises the question as to the original head of the valley (Nerepis
River/Back Creek), and here again I think the answer is fairly
clear. This same valley extends up the Northwest Oromocto, (cut-
ting across the Forks near the low hills on the south) and up the
Yoho River to its head. But it did not end here, for it extended, I
believe, through a gap in the hills to the flat country at the source
of Gardner's Creek, through Lake George and the Pokiok, and into
the St. John, and this ancient and important valley we may well
call from its modern remnant, The Nerepisian Valley.

Ganong recognized that he was boldly speculating, noting: "The conclusions
drawn from the facts stated are of course largely tentative. I regard them
as in the highest degree probable, but much study is still needed before
they can be either fully confirmed or definitely disproved."[6]

His first field trip of the summer concluded, Ganong parted ways with
Hay. He promptly travelled to Fredericton and caught the train to Newburg
Junction, near Woodstock, where Professor Arthur Pierce waited to join
him for the first of many field trips. Never one to squander time, Ganong
took notes on the Keswick River watershed from the train, admitting: "The
method is not ideal but the trains in that valley do not move at a rate to
render such study quite impossible, especially when several trips are made
to supplement one another in conjunction with the use of best maps."[7]

His observations of the landscape led Ganong to see the lower section
of the Saint John River as having been a continuation of the Keswick River

W.F. Ganong preparing to pole his canoe up Little Tobique River

(NBM, William Francis Ganong Collection, Image 1987-17-1219-6)

in the ancient past. As he studied the Keswick and its valley, he speculated about its relationship with the Nashwaak and Southwest Miramichi Rivers in preglacial times:

> *I have suggested the probability that the north and south parts of both the Nashwaak and the Miramichi, both of which lie in a direct line north from its present source, formerly flowed through this valley, and certainly its great size strongly sustains this conclusion. I believe that these three rivers lie in a single ancient valley, with large and important branches, forming the original head of all the St. John below it, and this we may call from its modern remnant, The Keswain Valley.*[8]

From Newburg Junction, Ganong and Pierce travelled to Perth Andover and immediately began the two-day trip up the Tobique River to the settlement at Nictau. Time was of the essence, so they acquired supplies and a canoe and immediately started to pole rather awkwardly up the unusually high waters of the Little Tobique before setting up camp.

They spent two days at Nictau Lake, remeasuring the elevations of the surrounding mountains and refining maps from Ganong's 1899 trip. His field notes from Saturday, August 8, 1903, describe one clear, cold day's activity: "made an early start for Mount Bailey..... It was a fine day for climbing, and we visited all the peaks, taking their heights and examined all ledges — but found no felsite."[9]

The approaching end of summer left little time for repeating prior fieldwork, so they pushed ahead down the Nepisiguit River to the mouth of the South Branch. It was first documented on the Franquelin-DeMeulles map of 1686. Crown surveyors and geologists had further mapped the river during the most recent survey in 1887, but Ganong felt the result was erroneous and fanciful. He had conducted a preliminary scouting of the branch during his field trips in 1898 and 1899, so he was familiar with its lower section. He described its navigation challenges in his 1903 notes, writing:

> One of the least known of all the wilderness parts of New Brunswick is that drained by the South Branch Nepisiguit. This is because that stream is practically not navigable for canoes from its mouth, while it is extremely difficult of access from any other direction.[10]

Low water made the two men's journey up the South Branch especially arduous. There was no poling but, instead, the continual push and tug of the fully loaded canoe around and over large boulders, through a narrow mountain ravine. Ganong described the gruelling struggle upriver and then overland:

> We dragged our canoe and load up for some ten miles (a mile or two above the Second Forks) and went the remainder of the distance on foot; afterwards we carried over from near Paradise Pond into the source of the Northwest, and descended that river to Newcastle.[11]

The South Branch Nepisiguit, above Paradise Pond, June 2011 and August 1903

(Bottom: NBM, William Francis Ganong Collection, Image 1987-17-1219-61)

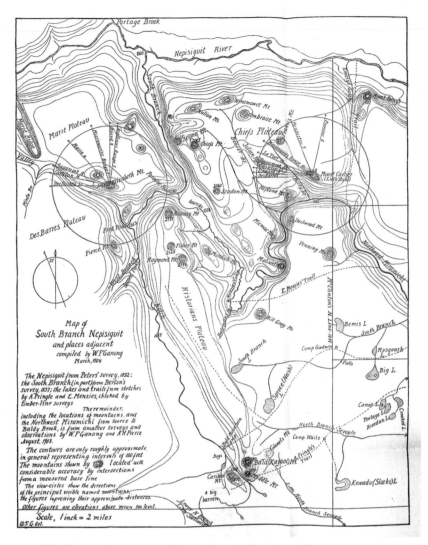

W.F. Ganong's 1903 map of South Branch Nepsiguit River (PANB-MC1799)

They established a base camp they fondly called Camp Seelye at Paradise
Pond and began several days of studying the physiography of the South
Branch Nepisiguit and its surrounding forest and mountains. The pond,
named by Ganong after the tranquil pool at Smith College, was the only
quiet water on the river. It was full of gigantic trout "of so wondrous size,
beauty, number and voracity, that a man doth danger his name for truth
if he but tell the fact concerning them."[12] Pierce's diary entry supports
Ganong's fish story and his conservation ethic. "G. used the troll and pulled

Paradise Pond, South Branch Nepisiguit River, June 2011 and August 1903

(Bottom: NBM, William Francis Ganong Collection, Image 1987-17-1219-64)

in 5 or 6 fine fellows from 12 to 19 in. long," he noted, "putting back all but one for the pot."[13]

Three aspects of the river impressed Ganong: its gradual change from deadwater to extreme turbulence, the high surrounding hills, and the close proximity to the headwaters of other rivers. Ganong and Pierce followed the South Branch from Paradise Pond to the base of Big Bald Mountain to determine the headwaters. Ganong noted that it was known in Mi'kmaq as Kagoot and was the highest and most prominent peak. A close growth of heath, bushes, and lichens, intersected everywhere by caribou trails, covered its slopes. Above the tree line, they found caribou antlers amid the lichen and moss. When they reached the summit to take elevation measurements and triangulate with other peaks, Ganong realized that the South Branch Nepisiguit had its source in the same central highlands area as the Sevogle River and the Lower North Branch Little Southwest Miramichi River.

Within the barrens in these highlands, the South Branch progressed sluggishly northward before flowing between Mount Elizabeth and the mountains of the Historians Range. From that point on, it embarked on a continuous tumble over the boulder-strewn channel to the Nepisiguit River. Ganong estimated that some sections of the South Branch dropped seventy-five feet per mile, more than fourteen metres per kilometre. With the exception of Paradise Pond, the river was a wild mountain torrent so rough, he noted, "its roar can be heard far back upon the hills, where it forms the most characteristic sound of the region."[14] He also observed two westward-branching tributaries that he would return to explore on later trips.

Before returning to their base camp at Paradise Pond, Ganong made numerous climbs to nearby mountains, taking measurements of their heights, triangulating them with other peaks, and piecing together their relationship to the Nepisiguit, Upsalquitch, and Miramichi watersheds. Ganong called the region the grandest and roughest mountain region in the province, writing that it was "indeed one of the purest joys of life to stride in full-pulsing health on glorious summer days over such elevated places as this, where the eye may revel in the spacious distances."[15]

Satisfied with their investigations, Ganong and Pierce left Paradise Pond on August 27 and followed a small brook up through the valley between Mount Scudon and Mount Hannay, bound for the headwaters of the Northwest Miramichi. They had to haul all their supplies and equipment

Nick Guitard in 2012 and W.F. Ganong in 1903
on the summit of Big Bald Mountain

Arthur Pierce carrying gear from the South Branch Nepisiguit
River to the headwaters of the Northwest Miramichi River

up to the watershed divide and then return to carry their canoe through
alders and deadfalls to the deadwater that fed both watersheds. Pierce
wrote in his diary: "Floated canoe & waded for only short distance before
coming to woods where windfalls compelled us to carry 1/3m..... At 5
P.M. I was that played out that I begged for a stop and we camped by the
stream with good prospects ahead."[16]

Making headway through these headwaters certainly tested their
resolve. The nights were so cold at this elevation that a layer of ice coated
the water in their pail, and their socks and boots required a fire to warm
them before wearing. Ganong was tenacious, forever pushing the pace,
and at the end of exhausting days he always found enough energy to climb
the nearest mountain for observations or to determine the physiographic
characteristics of the region. An exhausted Pierce commented: "He is
utterly tireless & tramps and surveys all the time."[17]

The lack of maps for the upper Northwest Miramichi compelled Ganong
to gather as much detail as possible while in the watershed. He noted
that from Mount Cartier to its confluence with Glory Hole Brook, the

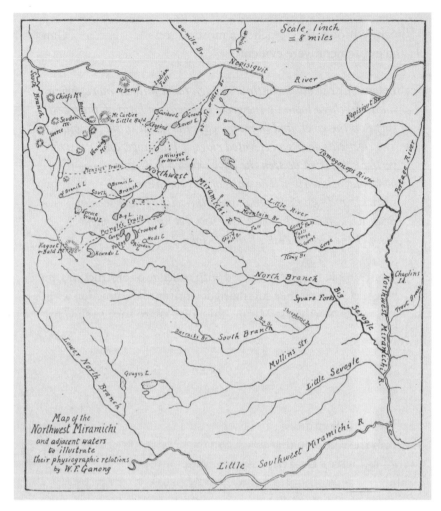

W.F. Ganong's 1903 map of the Northwest Miramichi River (PANB-MC1799)

Northwest Miramichi broadened and quickened, with several brooks joining the river at a location aptly called the Forks. Just above the Glory Hole, the river crossed its first vertical ledge, changing into a turbulent river with several waterfalls. The two men had much portaging to do as the river cut into the bedrock, forming deep gorges. Ganong considered this section of the Northwest Miramichi to be postglacial, whereas he classified the section above Glory Hole Brook and the section below Stony Brook as preglacial. He speculated that this section of the river had been turned away from its original course by glacial debris, and forced to find an alternative course, forming this newer, more turbulent section. Just above Stony Brook, they reached a most impressive sight, and Ganong's awe and excitement were evident:

> *Below this the river continues rough for a mile or more, when suddenly there loom up the great cliffs at the head of the finest gorge on the river, and in many ways the finest in the Province. The river cuts across an elevated ridge of hill range, and above the vertical cliffs can be seen the lofty wooded hills extending off on both sides of the river. The walls of this gorge are almost perfectly vertical, and rise higher than any other cliffs I have seen in New Brunswick, nearly, I should say, 200 feet, and much higher than those of the Grand Falls of the St. John.[18]*

Below Stony Brook, the river widened with no ledge or obstructions, making it much easier to canoe. They continued downriver to the junction with Little River where the Northwest Miramichi took a sharp turn to the northeast then flowed in a wide, sweeping arc back to the south. Ganong interpreted this northeast diversion as the river's ancient course to the Nepisiguit, a course altered by glacial action that forced the river southward.

Below Portage Brook, the river flowed through broad terraces and flood plains in a relatively straight course dotted with small islands until it met the Little Southwest Miramichi at Red Bank. Their final day on the river from the settlement at Wayerton to Newcastle was enjoyable if not relaxing, as Pierce's final trip entry reflects:

> *Arose at 5. and got started as soon as possible for the 25 m. run to Newcastle. Good running at start, then 1/4m. shoals where we waded. Then paddling & poling alternately we reached Redbank at noon.... About 3.30–6.30 paddling with wind behind, the last 14 ms. Beautiful day. Supper and night with Dr. Nickelson.[19]*

A warm meal and great Miramichi hospitality completed a very hectic summer of physiographic explorations of the North Branch Oromocto River, the South Branch Nepisiguit River, and the Northwest Miramichi River.

More than a century after Ganong, I visited the South Branch Nepisiguit with friends Rod O'Connell and Karl Branch. We could hear the roar of the river from the old logging road as we walked along from Adams Brook to Paradise Pond. At times the sound was so deafening that I dropped

Lower Gorge of the Northwest Miramichi River, August 2012 and
September 1903 (Bottom: NBM, William Francis Ganong Collection, Image 1987-17-1219-95)

down through the woods to see if it was a waterfall, only to find the river crashing over and around large boulders. The decline was so great that I could actually see the downward slope of the river when I set up my camera to take photos.

In more recent times, the peak of Big Bald Mountain has been extensively damaged by all-terrain vehicles tearing up the protective moss. Access to the top is by a road constructed to allow the construction and maintenance of radio towers.

Later that summer, I drove out the Fraser Burchill logging road from Wayerton, determined to get as close to the headwaters of the Northwest Miramichi as possible. The headwater comes from two branches. The South Branch has its source in a series of small lakes to the north of Big Bald Mountain, near the head of the Sevogle River and the South Branch Nepisiguit River. The Northwest Miramichi begins in the Historian Range, high in the central plateau. After several wrong turns and a walk through a clear-cut and meadow, I finally made it to the river. Wet and tired, I shot several pictures and returned to my friend Brian Mercier's fishing camp for a well-deserved steak and beer.

Looking west up the Long Deadwater towards Gover Mountain,
May 2012 and July 1904 (Bottom: NBM, William Francis Ganong Collection, Image 1987-17-1219-158)

10

The Ancient Land

Walkemik Basin to Renous River, Summer 1904

The spirit may come into sympathetic touch with all benignant nature, and the mind finds satisfaction in the pride of accomplishment as it solves the problems of the construction of this ancient land.

— W.F. GANONG[1]

In the summer of 1904, Ganong and Arthur Pierce once again travelled up the Tobique River, intending to continue the physiographic study of the Miramichi River watershed by returning to the central highlands. Ganong considered the watershed of the central plateau to be the oldest in the province, noting: "so far as our present river systems are concerned, this central plateau is the primitive or original watershed of the province.[2]

From Riley Brook they travelled overland to Portage Lake, and Ganong yet again measured its depth and temperature, as well as the elevation of the lake and surrounding hills to validate earlier measurements. He examined its relationship with the other lakes that form the Negoot group before hiking over the divide to the Miramichi watershed and their base camp. It was a similarly arduous route to the 1901 trip, but this time the two men did the work by themselves.

We portaged from Portage Lake, Tobique, without guides or other aid, by way of Hind Lake and other lakes and ponds of Adder Lake Stream to Upper Graham Plains and thence to Gover Lake,

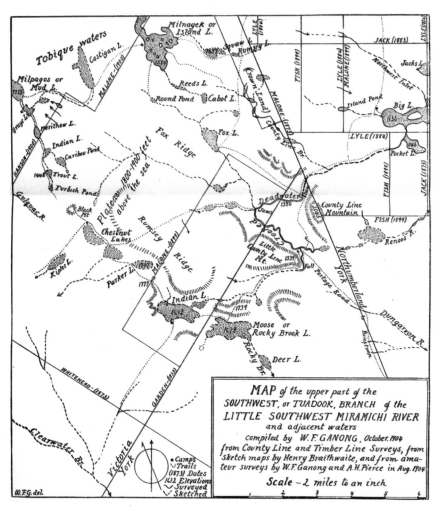

Map labels (as visible): Tobique waters · Costigan L. · Milnagek or Island L. · Milpagos or Mud L. · Reeds L. · Round Pond · Cabot L. · Fox Ridge · Fox L. · MALONE (1900) · Indian L. · Caribou Pond · Trout L. · Furbush Pond · Plateau 1800–1900 feet above the sea · Black Mt. · Chestnut Lakes · Rumsey Ridge · Kipsel L. · Parker L. · Indian L. · Moose or Rocky Brook L. · Deer L. · Rocky Br. · Deadwater · County Line Mountain · Little County Line Mt. 1331 · Fall Portage Road · York · Northumberland · Renous R. · FISH (1899) · JACK (1873) · Pocket L. · LYLE (1884) · Big L. · Island Pond · Jacks I. · Northwest Inlet · JACK (1883) · Squaw Rumsey I. · Coldwater Br. · Clearwater Br. · Whitehead (1873) · Victoria · York · Garden (1872) · Dungarvon R. · Boisetown

MAP of the upper part of the SOUTHWEST, or TUADOOK, BRANCH of the LITTLE SOUTHWEST MIRAMICHI RIVER and adjacent waters compiled by W.F. GANONG, October 1904 from County Line and Timber Line Surveys, from Sketch maps by Henry Braithwaite, and from amateur surveys by W.F. Ganong and A.H. Pierce in Aug. 1904

Scale – 2 miles to an inch

* Camps · Trails · (1873) Dates · 1412 Elevations · Surveyed · Sketched

W.F. Ganong's 1904 map of the Southwest, or Tuadook, branch of the
Little Southwest Miramichi River (currently known as West Branch Little
Southwest Miramichi) (PANB-MC1799)

*where we established our base camp. Afterwards we descended the
Upper North Branch, studied briefly the Crooked Deadwater and
Indian Lake Region, and came out by the Renous.*[3]

They spent July 14 to August 15 surveying and taking copious field notes
on an area that "because of its remoteness and difficulty of access, has
been hitherto little visited, scantly surveyed, hardly at all mentioned in
print, and wholly understudied by any scientific men."[4] Ganong revisited

Patchell Brook to refine his earlier maps and ascended Thunder Mountain, triangulating the mountain's position with other peaks. From the top of Gover Mountain, he determined the best route to portage from the Walkemik Basin to the Crooked Deadwater. He found the Walkemik a typical basin, hollowed out from the great central plateau by postglacial action. Its boulder-strewn surface had obstructed drainage, creating a series of long deadwaters at the edge of the elevated plateau and forming the headwaters of the Little Southwest Miramichi.

Wild game was plentiful in this remote part of the province, and the two explorers saw moose and deer almost every day. One evening, as they were doing fieldwork, they were visited by one of the caribou prevalent in the central highlands at the time. Pierce recorded that the caribou "very tamely strolled along the shore as we searched. She looked at us but gave us little heed."[5]

Both men were fully aware that any accident in the remote wilderness could jeopardize their lives and the field trip. Though usually judicious in their actions, occasional accidents did happen. Ganong injured himself on July 25 when, as Pierce later reported, he "undertook to leap an in-make of water, landed on his toes and broke a tendon or something in his left calf. For a time things looked dubious."[6] Despite considerable discomfort, Ganong continued his scientific studies. Six days later he allowed himself a rest on his friend's birthday. Pierce's journal entry for July 30 paints a compelling picture of the men relaxing in an idyllic wilderness setting. It also shows how much Ganong appreciated his friend's presence on the trip:

> *The morning is crisp and sunny — a capital drying-out day. Everything is hung about or spread about, and beans & apples are on the fire. It is just the glorious day we longed for — plenty of fine air and hot sun and no flies yet of any description. It seems like Sunday — morning spent not too strenuously in putting up tent, getting boughs, napping etc. Then a big birthday dinner of ham, soup, hardtack, sweet chocolate, nuts, raisins & tea. Then came mending — leisurely conducted — each putting huge canvas patches on our shirt sleeves. Then a further nap & then supper of beans, flap-jacks, & cocoa. Then a birthday paddle on the Lake, G. insisting that I be passenger (thought [sic] I paddled most of the way). A mess of fine trout from the inlet and a little prowling for game. 2 bull moose, 3 cows, 1 buck. Then about 9 a cheerful fire and*

Arthur Pierce on his birthday in the Gover Lake Region, July 30, 1904

(NBM, William Francis Ganong Collection, Image 1987-17-1219-129)

a brown sugar, birthday toddy by way of a closing celebration. It was a capital way to pass a birthday & G. did everything possible to make the day a notable one for me.[7]

Ganong had uncovered little that was unexpected, and though satisfied that he had examined the area thoroughly, he was somewhat disappointed, noting: "The mind of man is so constructed that it is prone to imagine things rare and choice in places remote and hard to reach, and so we looked forward hopefully to finding something especially worthy of note in these distant parts."[8]

Next, Ganong and Pierce set out overland through an area Ganong had investigated three years before, carrying their equipment and supplies along narrow hunting and game trails from Gover Lake to the Crooked Deadwater. It was an exhausting trek. Ganong noted that this portion of the watershed extended for miles, winding through a flat, boggy basin dominated by spruce

W.F. Ganong knee-deep in the headwaters of the Long Deadwater, 1904

(NBM, William Francis Ganong Collection, Image 1987-17-1219-155)

and cedar. The Deadwaters intrigued Ganong "because of their anomalous position directly across the general river trend of this region."[9] As well, the Crooked Deadwater contained the Jaws, a narrow channel with a sharp central ridge resembling the back of a horse that ran perpendicular to the water flow. His trip report showed that he remained mystified:

> But the question as to their mode of origin is one of the most puzzling in all the range of New Brunswick physiography, and I sought in vain during my twin visits, 1901 and 1904, to find some clue to its solution. Since these two rivers cut directly across at right angles to the general original river-trend of this region, which is plainly northwest-southeast, and since these valleys are obviously newer than the more ancient series, I can only surmise that they owe their origin to some local causes, whether softer rocks, fault lines, ancient glacial phenomena, or other, is still to be determined.[10]

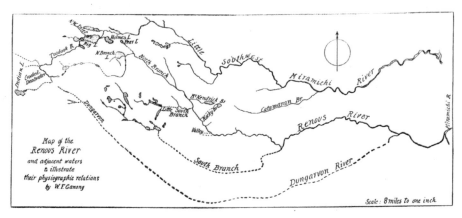

W.F. Ganong's 1904 map of the Renous River (PANB-MC1799)

When they finally reached the Crooked Deadwater, Pierce stayed behind to rest and set up camp for the evening. The ever-energetic Ganong set off to find a canoe, which Henry Braithwaite had assured him was left in the area, and to explore the watershed. Facing time constraints in order to meet Braithwaite at his Holmes Lake camp, Ganong and Pierce wasted no time the next morning and began canoeing downriver. They missed Braithwaite but used one of his portage trails to carry their gear and canoe across the divide to North Renous Lake. Ganong took the opportunity to remeasure elevations for the lake and surrounding hills, and spent three days documenting the area's physiography.

Ganong noted that the North Renous Lake is an anomaly because the inlet from the river that feeds it is very close to the outlet of the lake. He speculated that the inlet and outlet were once contiguous parts of a river that flowed beside the lake, and that postglacial influences had tipped the lake gently enough to join the river to the lake, leaving the inlet and outlet close to each other. Always the explorer, Ganong poled the canoe up the inlet until he was forced to leave it behind and hike through the alders in order to detail the features of the meadow and hills to the west.

The friends' easy lake paddling ended as they canoed down to the North Branch Renous River. It was an experience that would test their strength, determination, and friendship. Ganong and Pierce had been warned that the North Branch Renous River would be difficult to canoe, but just before leaving Braithwaite's camp on Holmes Lake, a horseback rider inspecting Lynch's camps assured them that although they might have "to get out once [or] twice," it was easily navigable. "Now this was decidedly cheering news

The boulder-laden North Branch Renous River, 1904

(NBM, William Francis Ganong Collection, Image 987-17-1219-176)

since we had looked for the greatest of difficulties," Pierce noted in his diary, "and were expecting to allow 10 days to get down." He and Ganong were somewhat incredulous, but, Pierce wrote, "we are much raised in hopes and our spirits are correspondingly bright."[11]

As predicted, the upper part of the river was relatively easy to navigate. In several places low water forced them to line the canoe around boulders, but they considered this easier than portaging. Below its confluence with the Little North Branch, however, the North Branch crossed a belt of granite and turned into a nightmare of falls and rapids. Ganong's report to the Natural History Society described the river's transition from placid to rough:

> For a mile below the Little South Branch the river continues open,
> pleasant and smooth; and then abruptly its bed becomes choked
> with great numbers of huge boulders and acquires much fall, which

North Branch Renous River, July 2011

conditions continue, with few and only local intermissions, down to within two miles of the Main South Branch, making this part of the river extremely difficult for canoe navigation, particularly at low water. The fall in this distance, 14½ miles is some 603 feet, an average of over 41 feet per mile. This part of the Renous is without doubt the roughest piece of river of its size and length, at least in which the roughness is due to boulders, in New Brunswick.[12]

While Ganong's report of the rough stretch of the Renous gave no indication of discouragement, Pierce's journals give a more emotional account. He recalled that the river:

started in with boulders, then more boulders & bigger boulders, strewn in the most fiendish & diabolical intricacy that the malevolent one himself could devise. It was tug & pull & lift and squirm, all the while slipping & sliding, wrenching the entire body & making one wonder what the object of it all was anyway. Nothing in the South Branch of the Nepisiguit can compare with this strip of boulder country.[13]

Renous River above McGraw Brook, July 2011

The experience had a profound effect on Pierce, pushing him to exhaustion. Even the copper wire that he used to reattach the tips of his shoes wore through completely. So gruelling was the river that Pierce began to question why he had ever agreed to accompany Ganong on another field trip, noting: "I cursed and swore I would never be caught doing this sort of thing again."[14]

Fortunately, the next day they entered the main Renous River, where canoeing became much easier over sandy riverbed and small islands and sandbars dotted calm waters. Downriver, towards the Southwest Miramichi, the landscape spread out on either side, forming terraces and flood plains.

The 1904 field trip season ended at Beaubears Island, and Ganong first began measuring the recession of the shoreline along the eastern coast of the province. He and Pierce used an existing fence line on the island as a baseline, so he could record changes that he saw as proof, "that New Brunswick is slowly sinking beneath the sea."[15]

The summer's field trips had been a success for Ganong. He determined that, except for the lake, the Renous river system was unchanged by the effects of glacial action, a condition unique among the rivers he had so far explored. He speculated that the Renous had formed the preglacial headwaters of the Southwest Miramichi and had been altered by the glaciers. From this trip, he produced the first detailed, reliable map of

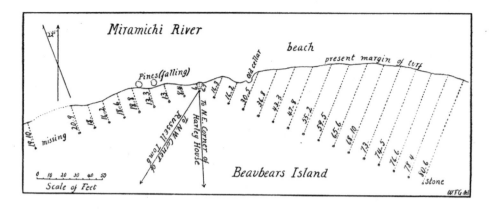

W.F. Ganong's 1904 map of Beaubears Island (PANB-MC1799)

the North Branch Renous River with readings taken by compass from a canoe and the help of "a very detailed and valuable sketch map sent me by Mr. Henry Braithwaite."[16] His report also noted that additional work was required to determine the relationship of the north branch of the Little Southwest Miramichi to the Tobique River, sowing the seeds of the following year's fieldwork.

Before leaving Newcastle he headed for Chatham and collected the recorded daily temperatures and barometric readings from the summer. Ganong would later compare these with his own measurements and those taken in Fredericton, his purpose being to determine exact elevations and mean temperature variations for areas where he had travelled.

11

Through Darkest New Brunswick

Central Highlands and Miscou Island, Summer 1905

Having the greatest respect for the conclusions of experts, I am ready to believe they are probably right, but must hold my opinion in abeyance until their material is worked over by other experts; for it is only after the acquisition of "impersonal validity" that such conclusions can be accepted as science.

— W.F. GANONG[1]

In his quest to understand and map the topography of the province's central highlands, Ganong planned an ambitious wilderness trek across the most remote section of the province to start the summer of 1905. With Arthur Pierce, he would conduct surveys, record physiographical features, and map as much as possible of the region from Portage Lake to the town of Bathurst. Ganong later referred to this uncharted terrain as "darkest New Brunswick." To complete the summer, the two men would canoe down the Tracadie River and north up the east coast of the Acadian Peninsula to Miscou Island.

The trip started with the familiar route up the Tobique River to the settlement of Riley Brook. Then, on July 8, a local guide took them by wagon several miles southwest through mountainous country to Bald Peak. They spent an extremely hot, mosquito-infested night before continuing the next morning to Portage Lake. The following day, they travelled out of the Tobique watershed by a hauling road, down the southeastern slope of the highlands, and into Walkemik Basin to the previous year's campsite

A canoe portage by horse and wagon from Nictau to Walkemik Basin, 1905

(NBM, William Francis Ganong Collection, Image 1987-17-1219-3)

at Gover Lake. From the lake they ascended Wilkinson Mountain to scout out the best possible route to Big Bald Mountain, and between the moose flies, mosquitoes, and heavy packs, it was tough going. The following day, the summer fieldwork began in earnest, which Ganong later summarized as follows:

> *From Gover Lake we went alone on foot, carrying provisions and outfit in packs, and making occasional side-excursions to Hough Lake and Skunk Lake, Half Moon Lake, Malone Pond, down the outlet of the latter to Cave Brook and the North Pole Branch, down this to near its mouth, across by portage road to the Lower North Branch, up this to the source of the eastern branch, north over the watershed to South Branch Nepisiguit and Kagoot, and down the South Branch Sevogle to Miramichi.*[2]

W.F. Ganong hiking through Walkemik Basin, 1905

(NBM, William Francis Ganong Collection, Image 1987-17-1222-5)

They finished the first day's hiking at Hough Lake, located in the shadows of Wilkinson Mountain and Mount Loggie. Progress with heavy packs full of provisions and scientific gear was slow, and Ganong's tireless energy once again tested his companion's fortitude and friendship. The companions hiked along game trails, clambering over deadfalls and trudging through a quagmire of wetlands as they headed northeast. At times the trails would lead to a deadwater or wetland, forcing them to backtrack or bushwhack around.

Early the next morning, they headed due north to Skunk Lake.[3] Dropping their heavy packs at the lake and taking only what was required, they set off on an almost twenty kilometre round-trip hike over the elevated plateau to Half Moon Lake and the headwaters of the West Branch North Pole Stream.[4] Ganong felt it was quite appropriate to call it the North Pole Branch of the Little Southwest Miramichi since it extended far northward and had notably cold water. Throughout the trek, he recorded the morning temperature each day. Later when comparing these readings to ones taken at Fredericton and Chatham, he noted that the temperature in the central highlands was, on average, nine degrees Fahrenheit colder.

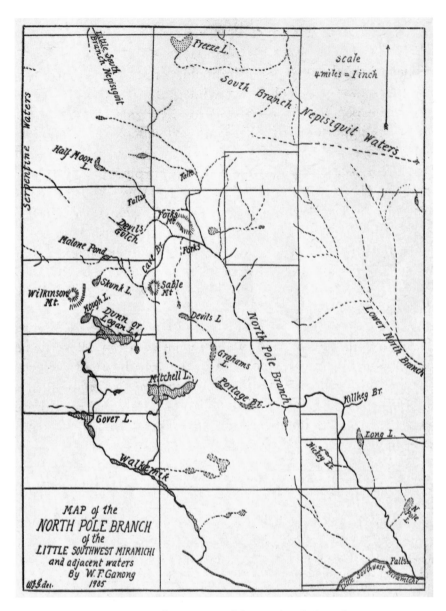

W.F. Ganong's 1905 map of the North Pole Branch
of the Little Southwest Miramichi River (PANB-MC1799)

North Pole Stream, May 2009

Ganong and Pierce used the evening at Skunk Lake to catch up on their journals and enjoy the rare treat of fresh lemonade. The following day they hiked to Malone Pond, then continued due east into the Cave Brook gorge, exploring the caves formed in its walls and reporting:

> *One side of this gorge is angularly concave while the other is an island the angles of which appear to fit into the concave side, showing that here at least the valley is a rift, though the stream has worn also little caves into the joints of the granite thus giving this stream its name.*[5]

Where the brook met the North Pole Stream, they decided not to venture up to the West Branch on this trip. Henry Braithwaite had said that its fast-flowing waters dropped almost forty-six metres over granite ledges from its source at Half Moon Lake, and Ganong had turned up no geological information about the watershed.[6] Instead, the two men continued with their plan and hiked south to the forks with the East Branch and then further down the Pole to within five kilometres of its confluence with the Little Southwest Miramichi. Ganong noted that much of the stretch

Little Sheephouse Falls, August 2012

below the forks was calm water with a sand and gravel bottom, making it an excellent stretch of water to canoe, except for a rough section in the final five kilometres called the Palisades. He concluded that this was a newer, postglacial channel, and that the original channel would have been farther east.

Ganong and Pierce crossed to the eastern side of the North Pole Stream on a hauling road and headed north along the ridge that separated it from the Lower North Branch Little Southwest Miramichi. Over the next few days they hiked up into the highlands towards Kagoot Stream. In this densely forested region they were compelled to camp beside the stream for an early start on the next day's trek to Big Bald Mountain. On the morning of July 20 they followed a direct line, at times wading through the ice-cold water of the Kagoot stream, with Ganong continually pushing the pace. When they finally reached the mountain, he immediately climbed to the summit for the second time in successive years to determine the elevation and document any notable features overlooked on the previous visit, leaving a somewhat disoriented Pierce to set up camp.

After a much-appreciated warmer night, Pierce's journal notes: "Started at 7, as usual, down whatever stream it may have been, probably the Little N. Br. Sevogle — the maps are faulty and contradictory."[7] In fact, they had found the South Branch Big Sevogle River, a region of the Miramichi watershed that was being actively lumbered. They finally had fairly decent hauling roads and trails to follow, though occasionally they were forced to push through thick brush and alders as they followed the river. Sketching crude field maps with every brook or stream they encountered, Ganong noted that the South Branch flowed over a gravel bed with little fall before reaching a section that narrowed where it became a swift shallow river.

Eventually they found themselves at the mouth of the Little Sheephouse Brook, which Ganong had been told featured a waterfall of substantial height and beauty. Pierce opted for a nap beside the river, while Ganong carried the camera up the brook in a disappointing search for Little Sheephouse Falls, which he later learned was "2 miles up & about 60 ft. high."[8]

They pressed on downriver, eventually arriving at the Square Forks, where Pierce headed to the nearby Sevogle fishing club and Ganong, true to his character, began preliminary physiographic studies. The explorers stayed with clubhouse keeper George Estey for two nights before heading north towards the Nepisiguit River. Pierce was much taken by Estey's candour and stories, and he wrote about the encounter in his journal:

> Then I went over to the Sevogle Club House and interviewed the keeper. He and his son Joe were just about to go out to the settlements. (George Estey, N. Esk, Sevogle P.O. N.B.) We walked out 7 m. put up at his house for the night, got bread & butter & beans & meat & for our supper & breakfast & were happy. We were highly entertained by Mr. Estey's stories about dam building.[9]

In the early hours of July 27, they started for the Nepisiguit along a rough logging road that followed the Northwest Miramichi until it veered to the northwest, following the Tomogonops River away from their destination. They then began a hike by compass in the rain that Pierce described as "simply frightful, through almost impassable burnt land, through cedar thickets & through alders."[10] Just beyond the divide in the land they found an old portage road to the Nepisiguit. It was a welcome relief to reach the river and they immediately headed downriver in the pouring rain, mistakenly believing they were almost at their camping site at the Narrows. Pierce later wrote:

> Instead we were 3 ms. above them. We trudged along the beaches and soon it began to thunder & rain but we moved right along with rubber coats as yesterday. About 1 m. perhaps below the Narrows we

Arthur Pierce poling on the Tracadie River, 1905

(NBM, William Francis Ganong Collection, Image 1987-17-1223-27)

camped wet to the skin. But we were at an old camping place &
managed to get wood enough to start a huge birch fire. We ate supper
in the rain and went to bed in the rain but it stopped storming soon
though it did not clear. Drops from the trees were falling most of
the night. It was a great comfort to be warm & dry in bed after
such a day.[11]

They were up at 4:30 a.m. the next day, and their luck had changed. After
hiking along the river on trails and an old tote road long used by lumbermen and First Nations, they met a wagon hauling supplies upriver from
Bathurst. Pierce described the encounter:

By good luck we met two boys driving an express wagon to the Club
House. They were much astonished and, as we learned later, not a
little frightened at our appearance, which must have been disqui-
eting on such a road since we had our rubber coats thrown over our
heads & packs. They took us for travelling musicians but soon took
our word for it that we were cruisers.[12]

The wagon drivers agreed to take the two men on the return trip, leaving Ganong and Pierce to walk to Pabineau Falls, where they rested and waited for the wagon to Bathurst.

After twenty days hiking through the wilderness, they arrived in Bathurst on July 28 and happily booked into Robertson Hotel to prepare for the next field trip, this time to the northeast tip of the province at Miscou Island. Rested, resupplied and with a canoe, they were taken overland by wagon to Bass River. From the Bass River they made their way up one of its tributaries, Curries Brook, to its headwaters. The companions carried their gear over a short portage into the headwaters of the blood-red Big Tracadie River, which, like other rivers in the Acadian Peninsula, was coloured by tannic acid from its source in peat bog wetlands. The slow, meandering river cut deeply into the soft soil, and Ganong found that intensive lumbering and spring log drives had eroded the river banks, making the river wider than it otherwise would have been.

Below an unusual V-shaped ravine where the Lord and Foy Brook joined the Big Tracadie River, the river widened and their pace picked up. "I took the pole today and by noon we had made 8 ms," Pierce wrote. "We found a glorious open sodded place for dinner and here we stopped until nearly 3. Then we started down again using once or twice the sail G. had rigged, no poling, paddling."[13]

Ganong found time to investigate the traditional Mi'kmaq portage route at Portage River then sailed into Tracadie harbour and set camp on a grassy saltwater beach. Before heading up the coast to Miscou Island, he explored the sheltered waters behind sandy barrier islands and documented the physiography of the Pokemouche River. He noted the effects of storms on the sandy coastline and the rich bounty of peat moss all along the peninsula. Ganong sketched and mapped the ever-changing dunes, fascinated by the unique natural history.

> *Those who have knowledge of the physical geography of New Brunswick are aware that our North Shore, all the way from Miscou to Buctouche [sic], is fringed by a line of long, low, narrow sand islands; but few have any idea of their great scientific interest or know that they constitute the finest example of this particular physiographic structure found anywhere upon the American coast north of New Jersey.*[14]

Storm over Shippegan Lighthouse, August 2012

Looking across Frye's Pond, Miscou Island, August 2012

Moving towards the northeast, exploring the shoreline of Shippegan and Lameque Island, they eventually reached Miscou Island, where Ganong obviously found many captivating aspects, "an island curiously formed and forever in change, haunt of wild life and center of quiet scenic charm, storied of old, remote from progress, primitive in population."[15] He determined that the island was actually a series of small islands linked by sandbars and bogs. He made a detailed map and documented what he learned of its rich human and natural history. Notable among his finds were fossilized walrus bones discovered in a heavily wooded area almost half a kilometre from shore. Ganong gathered the bones and shipped the finest pieces to the Natural History Society collection in Saint John.

Through thoughtful analysis of the island's geology, Ganong surmised that it was the end of the New Brunswick portion of the Appalachian Range, which tilts downward until it finally disappears below the surf at Miscou. In the central section of the island, he documented a unique geological formation called the Grande Plaine. The large barren, stretching from the southwest tip through to the northeast, was an anomaly in that the land on the plain appeared to be building up while the coast was sinking. He determined that this phenomenon did not occur in regular patterns but was produced by storm surges from the west. Ganong described the

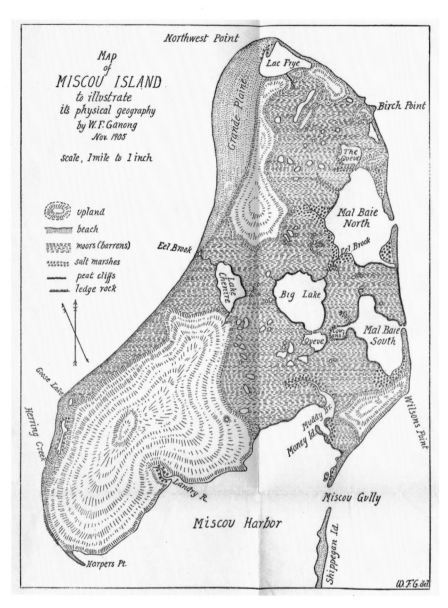

W.F. Ganong 1905 Map of Miscou Island (PANB-MC1799)

Ned Vibert and family, Miscou Island, 1905
(NBM, William Francis Ganong Collection, Image 1987-17-1222-47)

process: "In most places the sand is driven by the waves still higher, until, intermingled with driftwood, gravel, cobbles and occasional boulders brought from Gaspé by the ice, it is piled in ridges above high-tide mark."[16] Grasses bound the material together and, over time, the area became covered with shrubs and trees.

A second area of great interest to Ganong was the great barren that covered almost half of the island. Scattered throughout were small bogs and ponds as well as clusters of dwarfed spruce and tamarack, all held in place by a deep layer of several species of sphagnum moss. Since sphagnum can only grow in fresh water, Ganong concluded that the barren was formed when the island was much higher above sea level. After much analysis, he postulated that a protective elevated ridge once rimmed the barren

Pokeshaw Rock, Bay of Chaleur, Gloucester County, August 2012

but had slowly eroded. Over time, the sea infiltrated the eastern side of the island and transformed the freshwater ponds into saltwater lagoons.

Ganong was clearly delighted by this elegant example of the constant interplay of natural forces, later reporting:

> *Thus we see that physiographically Miscou is one of the most interesting of the parts of New Brunswick. It represents an area of unstable equilibrium and owes its characters to delicate adjustments of level. Nowhere in the province are topographical changes in more active progress or their operation so clear.*[17]

While on the island, he met frequently with local residents to learn about their culture and the history of the island. A mixture of Scottish and Acadian settlers had been fishing and farming there for almost hundred years, and Pierce praised their hospitality, writing: "We are living well, herring & potatoes & toast for breakfast, eggs & beans for dinner and flaps for supper."[18]

They reluctantly left the island, heading west along the coast road and stopping in Pokeshaw to examine the geology and the effects of storms on the headlands. Their long summer of field trips for 1905 ended in Bathurst in early September.

12

Strikingly Wild

The Square Forks Big Sevogle River Revisited, Summer 1906

The Sevogle is our most perfect wilderness river, by far the largest in New Brunswick that is wholly unsettled from source to mouth. It is also one of the least known and poorest mapped, for the reason, no doubt, that all its branches are well-nigh un-navigable, because of their roughness, for canoe, while none of them afford through routes of travel into other streams.

—W.F. GANONG[1]

Ganong began the summer field trip for 1906 travelling overland by wagon from Newcastle to Gaugas Lake, part of the headwaters of the Lower North Branch of the Little Southwest Miramichi River. Much like the previous year's excursion, the trip consisted of hiking along the most isolated valleys and hills of the Miramichi watershed to record relevant features of its physiography. Once again, his companion was Arthur Pierce, who seemed to have forgotten his determination the previous summer not to hike the wilderness with Ganong again.

> We went on foot (carrying our outfit in packs, and without guides or other aid) from Guagus Lake to and up the Branch, across by the upper portage road to the North Pole Branch, to the headwaters of that stream, Freeze Lake, the source of this Branch, Kagoot, the North Branch Sevogle, and down that stream to Square Forks and the Northwest Miramichi. From this route we made side excursions in various places.[2]

A stream feeding the Lower North Branch Little Southwest Miramichi River, May 2009

The two men used their time at Gaugas Lake to prepare for the fieldwork and mail last-minute post. Ganong also measured the lake's depth and dimensions, examined the shallows, explored its inlet and outlet, and studied the surrounding meadows and barrens. He noted that little was known about this part of the watershed, in particular its geological or physiographic details, although its forests had been widely harvested.

With exploration around the lake completed, they began hiking in earnest, first into the upper reaches of the Lower North Branch of the Little Southwest Miramichi. Moving north along overgrown portage trails and through thick alders and deadfalls, they worked their way towards the central plateau and the source of the river. Ganong reported numerous game trails leading into the river basin, an indication of excellent hunting grounds. One unanticipated challenge was flooding from beaver ponds, which forced them from their intended path on an already taxing hike.

The Lower North Branch Little Southwest Miramichi flowed southward between the Aspkwa Ridge and the Central Plateau. Its smooth course accelerated as it became narrower and the landscape more elevated. Eventually, the explorers began to climb into the central plateau, where several streams formed the headwaters. They climbed past cascades that plunged over the moss-covered escarpment to be swallowed by large boulders before reappearing farther down the side of the mountain.

In 1906, Ganong found sections of the region that were as yet untouched by logging operations. He took temperature readings as well as elevation measurements and, always the botanist, studied and documented the plant life, later noting that: "The vegetation of any given region viewed as a whole always exhibits a distinct general character or type determined by the two most fundamental of all ecological factors, temperature and precipitation."[3]

Ganong and Pierce trekked west over a trail into the East Branch North Pole Stream, an area that had not been part of their explorations the previous summer. Once in this watershed, Ganong learned that the upper reaches of the stream were not as he had expected:

> *In my note on the North Pole Branch, I ventured to surmise that the main stream above Forks Mountain would be found to wind quietly in a large basin. Nothing could be further from the truth.... On the contrary, ascending above Forks Mountain, the stream becomes swifter and swifter, until it is a mountain torrent, pouring down in cascades and falls through a granite gorge from its sources on the surface of the plateau.*[4]

Following the East Branch through dense undergrowth, they headed for Freeze Lake, considered by Ganong to be the most remote in the province. Located at the height of land between the Miramichi and Nepisiguit watersheds, it formed part of the headwaters of the South Branch Nepisiguit River. The going was extremely tough, with no maps and, worse yet, survey lines that terminated abruptly. Large beaver ponds also continued to obstruct their progress. Pierce wasn't having a good time and made no bones about it, but Ganong, as usual, was largely unaffected by the difficulties. Pierce's journal captured his feelings: "This is a wretched part of the country and the sooner out of it the better," he wrote. "Upon mentioning it jokingly G. said he would have spent a heap more time there had he thought I would be willing to do so."[5]

Twelve long days after leaving Gaugas Lake, the two men arrived at Freeze Lake. Most of the forest had burnt in recent fires, allowing open views. Pierce described their early morning departure for the lake, and his impression of its unusual character:

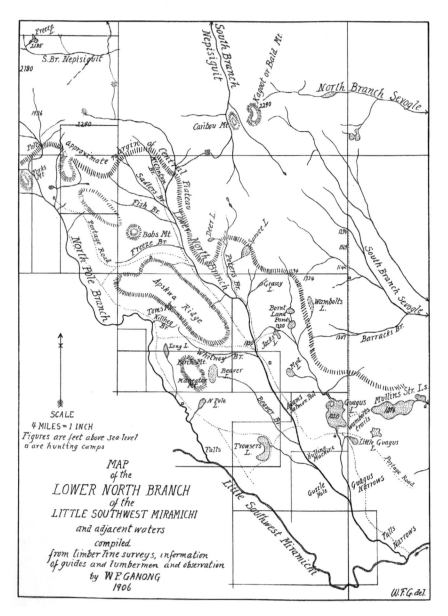

W.F. Ganong's 1906 map of the Lower North Branch
of the Little Southwest Miramichi (PANB-MC1799)

*July 17 up shortly after 4, started at 6 for Freeze Lake and in
short time came upon it — a low, boggy collection of water from
innumerable spring holes oozing out warmish water. A great moose
place judging by tracks — we came to the Lake in fact on a fine trail.
Now 8 A.M., we have circled about 2/3 about the place. . . . This is
the lake of which G. said encouragingly, "It's something to reach
the most inaccessible Lake in N.B." But what a lake!!*[6]

Hiking east from Freeze Lake along the Kagoot Stream, the pair eventually
crossed the headwaters of the South Branch Nepisiguit River, where even
Ganong seemed to become lost. Without the aid of reliable information
or survey lines, they found themselves unsure which stream they should
follow to reach their next destination at Big Bald Mountain. The wetlands
and barrens that formed the headwaters of several different watersheds
made it easy to become disoriented. At the end of one obviously exhausting
and confusing day, an exhausted Pierce summed up his feelings, writing:
"Heart has been jumping. Wish I had a pipe and wonder why in thunder
I ever came."[7] Ganong's dogged perseverance and unflagging optimism
eventually led them to the base of Big Bald Mountain, where he yet again
immediately headed for the summit to determine the best approach to the
headwaters of the North Branch Big Sevogle. Pierce set up camp beside the
South Branch Nepisiguit River where, despite the blackflies, he enjoyed
the singing of the hermit thrushes and robins. Ganong returned to camp
with enough extra energy that, after supper, Pierce recorded: "G. went
down and got a string of 13 trout."[8]

Following a compass bearing for the North Branch Big Sevogle River,
Pierce and Ganong headed east out of the Nepisiguit watershed. They
hiked along game trails around Big Bald Mountain until they reached the
headwaters of the Sevogle watershed just beyond Moose Lake. Ganong
described what they saw:

*The North Branch of Sevogle rises on the easterly slope of the
Kagoot, or Big Bald plateau, very near to a principal source of the
South Branch. [It] is at first a very sluggish dark-colored stream
of alternating deadwater and boulder rips, in slope and current.*[9]

They followed a promising lumber road, only to realize after a considerable
distance that it was leading them away from their intended direction. This

Freeze Lake October 2012 and July 1906

(Bottom: NBM, William Francis Ganong Collection, Image 1987-17-1222-61)

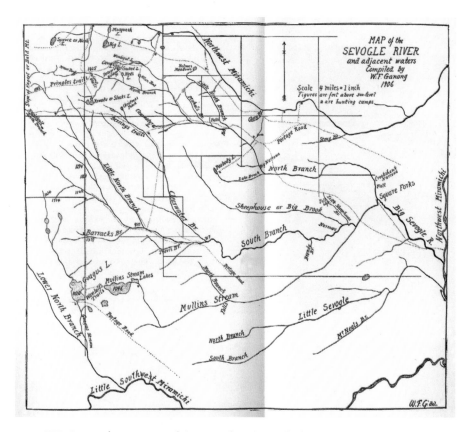

W.F. Ganong's 1906 map of the Sevogle River and adjacent waters (PANB-MC1799)

error forced them to use a compass and struggle through heavy woods to get back to the Sevogle. Although hiking along the river's edge was tiring, it proved enjoyable for its scenery and cooler air.

On July 27, just below the Big Narrows at the confluence of Peabody Brook and the Sevogle, they were downstream from one of the river's roughest stretches, "an irregular, wild postglacial gorge with a broken fall of four or five feet near its upper end."[10] The end of the trip was less than a day's walk away, none too soon for Pierce, who wrote in his journal: "Here we are, again at an old lumber camp which furnishes nothing but wood. Provisions are low. Flour & cornmeal flaps tonight. Passable. Last of cocoa."[11]

The next day, the thick forest below the camp forced them to hike along the riverbank and in the river. However, within an hour they had reached the top of Cruikshank Falls, with the Square Forks of the Sevogle less than a kilometre away.

Cruickshank Falls on the North Branch Big Sevogle River,
August 2012 and July 1906[12] (Bottom: NBM, William Francis Ganong Collection Image 1987-17-1222-69)

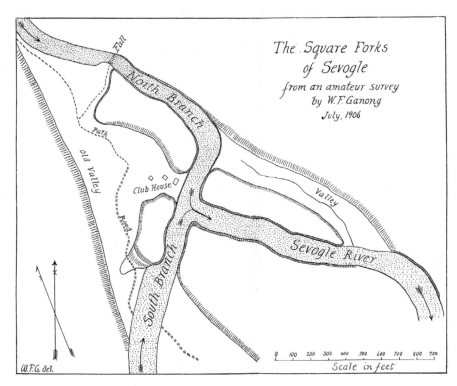

The Square Forks
of Sevogle
from an amateur survey
by W.F. Ganong
July, 1906

W.F. Ganong's 1906 map of the Square Forks Sevogle (PANB-MC1799)

Following on from his brief survey the previous summer, Ganong planned a prolonged stay at the Square Forks to study their formation further. On one side, the North Branch flowed through a narrowing in the bedrock, producing a high cliff, while on the opposite side, the South Branch flowed into the gorge through a much wider but equally high channel. Where the two branches met, they formed a large pool of swirling water before being forced out through a third narrow gorge at ninety degrees to their original path. This posed an intriguing geological and physiographic quandary, which Ganong was eager to explain.

> *Physiographically, it offers a curious problem in the unusual and anomalous arrangement whereby two large rivers come together, end to end, in the middle of a single straight gorge, and then turn their united waters at right angles through another. Geologically, it offers testimony, which I think is conclusive, of fluctuations in the glaciations of the province.*[13]

Looking down the Big Sevogle River from the Square Forks, 2012 and 1906

(Bottom: NBM, William Francis Ganong Collection, Image 1987-17-1222-70)

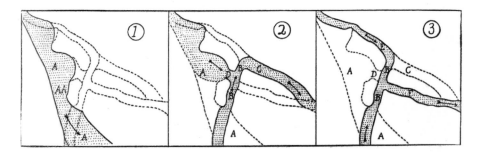

W.F. Ganong's diagrams explaining the formation
of the Square Forks (PANB-MC1799)

The men hiked the area around the falls, seeking explanations for its formation. At a bend in the North Branch below the falls, Ganong found a shallow, well-forested valley that he speculated was an earlier link between the North Branch and the Big Sevogle that lost its water source in the ancient past. He formulated a working hypothesis for the origin of the Square Forks, noting that there were two plausible reasons for the unusual formation. The first and least likely was a coincidence, while the second was that the gorge had been occupied by a single river in preglacial times.

His report to the Natural History Society explained the formation with the following theory, illustrated by a series of diagrams. He was careful to suggest that "a more thorough examination of the region, especially down river, where my knowledge is especially weak, may require its modification."[14]

> *First: Originally the two branches of the Sevogle did not come together in this region at all, but flowed independently northeastward....*

> *Second: In later times, under the influence of geological causes, a newer river worked back northeasterly from the Northwest Miramichi until it intersected the valleys, first the South then of the North Branch. Thus originated the main Sevogle and part of the North Branch, and it was this river, which occupied the "old Valley" of the map (A of Diagram). At this time the junction with it of the South Branch lay more to the southward, outside the limit of the accompanying map, where the South Branch had yet a great bend to the eastward. This stage is represented in the accompanying Diagram 1.*

A panoramic composite image showing the Square Forks
of the Big Sevogle River, August 2012

*Third: The glacial period arrived, and one of its effects was to choke
with drift the Sevogle valley below the original forks, and as well
the old valley at AA of the map, thus forcing the dammed rivers to
find new channels, and the Forks to lie in a new position. The lowest
outlet happened to lie in the position of the present Gorge BB, and
around by the present dry valley C, while the narrow rocks mass at
the present club house valley (D), afforded the lowest outlet for the
North Branch, thus locating the Forks there. Thus was established
the condition shown in Diagram 2.*

*Fourth: There ensued a change in the glacial continuity, whereby
both the old valleys, A and C, became choked, leaving the South
Branch, BB, unaffected, thereby forcing the North Branch and the
combined streams to find new channels, which they did, of course,
at the lowest points, which happened to lie where those parts of the*

two rivers are now running, viz., at E and F. Thus was established the present arrangement, represented by Diagram 3.[15]

With their first field trip of the summer finished, Ganong and Pierce continued overland to the settlement at Red Bank and a well-earned but brief respite in Newcastle. There, they gathered supplies before heading up the Bathurst-Chatham Portage road to the Tabusintac River. At the bridge spanning the Tabusintac, they put in their canoe, and Ganong began a physiographic study of the river. He had found the river on many early maps of the region, and he noted that it dropped eighteen to thirty metres through heavily wooded, terraced banks. Like the other rivers of the Acadian Peninsula, its headwaters lay in an extensive series of peat bogs that were preglacial in formation.

Ganong and Pierce continued downriver until they reached the first settlement at Stymiests Millstream, where the river flowed through expansive meadows before emptying into Miramichi Bay. From there, they returned to Newcastle to rest and clean up before boarding the train for the trip home.

Accompanied by Terry Gallant, I hiked along the Little North Branch Big Sevogle River and discovered a discrepancy in Ganong's report to the Natural History Society. He noted a large broken waterfall nearly eighteen metres (sixty feet) in height and described the stream just over a kilometre up from its mouth as large and clear. There are some small waterfalls and rapids about a kilometre above the mouth where the water has cut deeply into the plateau, but I did not locate any waterfall of that height. To his credit, Ganong was correct, however, about it being a clear stream, rising in a broad valley with several bogs and wetlands. After all, he did not actually explore this branch of the river but rather accepted information provided by reliable sources.

In August of 2012, along with Gary Tozer, I hiked down from Cruickshank Falls toward the forks, along the east side of the North Branch Big Sevogle River, and located its original channel. Following the gully through the forest, I emerged at the Big Sevogle River downstream from the forks. I later checked Google Maps, and this original channel can be easily identified. I made my way back to the North Branch and crossed the river. After changing into dry clothes I hiked downstream to the forks, where I shot a sequence of three images to produce the panoramic photo on pages 142-143.

13

A Challenging Puzzle

Southwest Miramichi Watershed, Summer 1908

As he explored the rivers, forests and mountains of his native
province his powers of observation were trained to accuracy,
his imagination was stirred and his mind stimulated to solve
the many mysteries and problems presented by the varied
phenomena of nature.

— J.C. WEBSTER[1]

The transition in the geology of the Southwest Miramichi River, above
and below Boiestown, presented yet another challenging physiographic
conundrum for Ganong. He was intrigued by the dramatic difference
"with which it is divided at Boiestown into two very dissimilar parts, as
unlike in history and conditions of settlement as in origin, geography and
geology."[2] This quandary enticed him back to what he called the second
most important river in New Brunswick, after the Saint John River.

Ganong's first field trip to the Southwest Miramichi River had been in
1890, and he did not return until he canoed the section from Boiestown
to Newcastle in 1907. He noted that the river's character was uniform
throughout and similar to others flowing within the region. He also noted
that the river had been settled below Boiestown, and its physiographic
characteristics well-mapped and documented.

In contrast, he found the upper section substantially different in
character:

*Above Boiestown it is mostly a rough narrow unsettled stream of
devious course through an elevated and broken country, complex*

Looking west up the Southwest Miramichi from
the bridge on Cains River Road, September 2014

*and puzzling in origin, character, and geological correlations, while
its principal branches come in at an abrupt angle from the north.*[3]

For this reason, he returned in the summer of 1908, once again with
Arthur Pierce. They started from the settlement at Juniper, located on the
North Branch Southwest Miramichi, just above the forks with the South
Branch. It was an ideal place to put in, near the central highlands of the
province. Nearby was the major watershed divide, with the Becaguimec
Stream running into the Saint John River and the South Branch into the
Miramichi system.

For this demanding field trip, Ganong focused on a physiographic study
of the North Branch Southwest Miramichi, as well as the headwaters of
the Wapske and Gaugas Rivers of the Tobique watershed. The section of
the Southwest Miramichi from the forks at Juniper to its confluence with
the Taxis River at Boiestown ran through beautiful wooded hills with some
of the finest river scenery in the province. Flowing swiftly over a gravel
bottom dotted by the occasional boulder, the river was easily navigable
by canoe, except for the Burnthill Rapids. Ganong noted that the major
tributaries, such as Clearwater, Sisters, and Rocky brooks, run in parallel
paths on the northern slope, cutting deep valleys through hilly country

W.F. Ganong's 1908 map of the upper part and branches of the main Southwest Miramichi and adjacent waters (PANB-MC1799)

to meet the main river at right angles. In contrast, the tributaries on the south bank tended to run parallel to the main river.

Using Barter's Hotel in Juniper, as their base, Pierce and Ganong first scouted the South Branch to its source near the divide in the land with the Saint John River. As well, Ganong studied the considerable meadow that extends for several miles around the settlement, before pushing northward by canoe on the North Branch. Paddling the languid lower section and poling the swifter sections, they travelled upstream to Bedel Brook. It's clear from Ganong's notes that, like most of his field trips, this excursion covered a vast area of the Southwest Miramichi watershed:

I went by canoe from Barters to above Bedel Brook, and thence on foot, taking advantage of the portage roads and making many side excursions, to the head of the North Branch Deadwater. Thence we went by Lindsay Brook to River de Chute and the source of its east branch, over to Gulquac, and back to Beaver Lake, down Burnt Hill to the Glassville Portage, across by Beaver Brook Lakes to Clearwater, up this stream to above Red Stone Brook and back to Sisters Lakes and down the Sisters and Miramichi to Hayesville.[4]

Barter's Hotel (Farm), Juniper, 1908

(NBM, William Francis Ganong Collection, Image 1987-17-1223-136)

The North Branch watershed was well known to surveyors, as in 1844 the Corps of Royal Engineers had mapped it as a proposed military route from Halifax to Quebec City. It was mapped again in 1846 and 1864 as part of the proposed Intercolonial Railway, and Ganong was aware of its role in the history of railroad building in New Brunswick.

Following a combination of lumbering and survey lines, Ganong studied the physiographic nature of the North Branch as they pushed farther towards the central highlands. He noted that, from its source to the forks, the branch dropped seventy-eight metres (256 feet). At times the terrain was strenuous, and the companions were forced to go through or around several wetlands. Trails that began promisingly would abruptly terminate, sometimes forcing a retreat to the previous trail and sometimes requiring them to bushwhack their way through. Pierce's notes make it clear that this was an arduous process:

> *Finally stopped about 1 without knowing exactly where we were. G. scouts after dinner and we leave loads and follow a freshly spotted trail to N.W. which ends after 1 m. in midair. Return, take packs, and following up Deadwater go on hauling road, in water and along typical marsh bank until we strike spotted trail.*[5]

North Branch Southwest Miramichi River, May 2011

Except for a few waterfalls where the encroaching hills forced the water through narrows, the river flowed through predominately open land, forming a series of extended wetlands with deep pools. They camped beside the North Branch deadwater and spent a few days taking barometric and temperature readings, with side excursions to the surrounding plateaus. Temperatures were low even in mid-summer, causing Pierce to write in his journal: "Was half frozen most of the night and it seemed as if I didn't sleep at all. Frost on boots, socks stiff, & ice in aluminum cups at 5 A.M."[6]

Continuing northeast from the barren, they entered a valley shadowed by high hills rising more than one hundred and fifty metres. In it were the shared headwaters of the North Branch, a tributary of the Southwest Miramichi, and Lindsay Brook, a tributary of the Wapske River, which in turn flowed into the Tobique River. Ganong determined that the upper section of the North Branch had once belonged to the Tobique watershed and had been turned away, not by glacial action but by the erosive power of water wearing down the softer rock on the southern side of the ridge.

Ganong was determined to complete his physiographic analysis of this remote section of the Tobique watershed. Having completed the Tobique River, the watershed surrounding the Little Tobique, the Right Hand Branch, and Negoot Lakes, what remained could be completed by making an easterly arc from the Wapske watershed to the Gulquac River. They continued northward over the watershed divide then down Lindsay

Gulquac Lake, 1908 (NBM, William Francis Ganong Collection, Image 1987-17-1223-55)

Brook to the Right Hand Branch River de Chute, heading overland from the river towards the headwaters of the Gulquac River.

The concluded exploration of the Tobique watershed did not allow Ganong to bask in his achievement. In fact, it inspired him to push the pace of the field trip. The companions immediately headed back over the divide in the land to the Southwest Miramichi. The heat was unusually oppressive, with occasional thunderstorms providing some relief, a marked contrast to the cold nights they had experienced earlier in the trip.

They set up camp near Beaver Lake and the headwaters of the North Branch Burnthill Brook, almost 427 metres above sea level. On one particular evening, before the pair had settled for the night, they had a strange and unexpected encounter that Pierce recorded in his journal.

While G. was down at the Lake about 5 heard voices and pres-
ently there appeared 5 men — probably French but with a patois
incomprehensible to me — who had come straight through the
woods from somewhere (they said Montreal via St. John) making
for Plaster Rock to seek work on the Transcontinental R.R. They
had been 3 days "in the bush" as one of them kept saying. They
had expected to find farms etc. I gave them directions for reaching
the Wapske Portage and soon G. came back and confirmed all I
had said. This seemed to reassure them and they started off much
to our relief, since we could hardly feed them and stay in the same
camp with them.[7]

Before departing, Ganong meticulously mapped Beaver Lake and determined its elevation and that of the surrounding meadows. The explorers
hiked down along the North Branch of Burnthill Brook to the Glassville
Portage, mapping the brook's course and recording its physiographic
characteristics. Then they hiked east to Beaver Brook Lake and the valley
of Big Clearwater Brook, the largest tributary of the upper section of
the Southwest Miramichi. With its source high above sea level in the
very heart of the highlands that separate the Little Southwest Miramichi
from the Southwest Miramichi, the Big Clearwater is also the wildest
of the tributaries. Wanting to explore farther up its headwaters to map
the terrain, Ganong and Pierce hiked north along its banks as far as Red
Stone Brook and then returned to follow the portage road overland to
Sisters Lake. Ganong's original intention had been to continue along the
portage east to Rocky Brook. Instead, he decided to follow the fast-flowing
Clearwater to the Southwest Miramichi, continue down along the river
to the mouth of Rocky Brook, and hike back up to its source. The change
in plans added considerable distance and time to an already exhausting
hike, putting additional stress on his relationship with Pierce.

The situation was exacerbated when the duo came upon an occupied
camp with welcoming smoke coming from the chimney. After several
weeks of solitude, Pierce was eager to cross the brook and introduce himself to the occupants, but even after weeks of bushwhacking through the
wilderness, Ganong was unwilling to do so, wanting to push the pace of
the field trip. Pierce's account of the occasion shows how the two men's
personalities differed:

Looking west up the Southwest Miramichi River
from Sisters Brook, July 2011 and August 1908

(Bottom: NBM, William Francis Ganong Collection, Image 1987-17-1223-111)

G. as usual was frightened at the thought of seeing anybody and made tracks hastily to disappear. I was mildly wrathy — in private — because encounters of that sort are my delight in the woods, and going down the road remarks framed themselves in my mind for G's reflection later.[8]

That evening there must have been a frank discussion concerning the remainder of the field trip. Earlier in the hike, Pierce had broached the subject of a substitute for the Dungarvan portion, as he was increasingly bothered by an irregular heartbeat. Ganong decided that they would not venture up Rocky Brook to the Dungarvan River the next day as originally planned but would make a much shorter hike directly to Fall Brook. For Ganong, it was critical to measure the falls to complete the previous year's fieldwork. Uncertainty about the exact height had thwarted his desire to establish which of the province's many waterfalls was the tallest:

While the Fall Brook Falls seems firmly established as the highest in all New Brunswick, I am told by Mr. J. W. Bailey that its pre-eminence is threatened by two very high falls which he has seen on the Merry Pitcher branch of the Big Salmon River in St. John County.[9]

One of the more interesting occurrences of that summer of 1908 — perhaps of all of Ganong's annual field trips — was the earthquake they experienced while breakfasting beside the river. As Pierce reported in his notes, they were unsure of the cause of the disturbance:

Yesterday morning while seated on logs eating breakfast 6-7 (?) there was a rumble resembling thunder to the N. accompanied by a distant trembling of the ground. We remarked that the rumble did not seem wholly like thunder, the rolling character being absent although the extent of the rumble was large. This P.M. we meet McKay who asks if we felt the earthquake yesterday morning. Said dishes were made to rattle.[10]

The epicentre of the earthquake was near Hartland and affected numerous communities all the way across the central portion of the province to Chatham. On August 8, 1908, the *Daily Gleaner* reported rumbles felt in

Fall Brook Falls, Southwest Miramichi River,
July 2014 and August 1908

(Bottom: NBM, William Francis Ganong Collection Image 1987-17-1223-118)

Sunset, Southwest Miramichi River, August 2012

the Fredericton area and "something along the line of seismic disturbance early last evening."[11]

Finished with his measurements and aware of Pierce's disinclination to prolong the trip, Ganong decided it was time to head for home. After a gruelling summer of fieldwork, carrying heavy packs with scientific equipment, camera, camping kit, and grub, Ganong must have been somewhat relieved as well. They proceeded to hike the hauling road along the river's edge to Hayesville and on to Boiestown. An exhausted Pierce would take a hiatus from Ganong's adventures until 1910, when he helped Ganong to finish mapping the Renous Lakes and South Branch Renous River and to continue the research they had begun in 1904 on coastal land regression at Beaubears Island.

William Laskey, Southwest Miramichi River, 1909

(NBM, William Francis Ganong Collection, Image 1987-17-1223-121)

14

Unfinished Business

The Southwest Miramichi, Summer 1909

As the years went on he seemed to get more enthusiastic and more tireless, until it was almost impossible for him to find anyone to keep pace with him in the woods.

— SUSAN B. GANONG[1]

Ganong returned to the upper section of the Southwest Miramichi River in the summer of 1909, determined to complete unfinished business. He wanted to remeasure the height of Fall Brook Falls by lowering a weighted cord from the top. He was also anxious to begin his exploration of Rocky Brook, which Pierce's health concerns deferred the previous summer. This time, his companion was young William Laskey of Fredericton.

While Ganong's measurement of the falls at thirty-three-and-a-half metres (110 feet) was more accurate than the previous year, he had resolved to make yet another attempt "using non-elastic wire and precautions which will ensure a result accurate within a foot."[2]

The second reason for this field trip was an analysis of Rocky Brook. Ganong later reported that the brook's lower section, where it had cut through the hills, flowed briskly over many rocks and boulders. Moving upriver, he noted a marked change above a high falls that dropped five-and-a-half-metres. Unlike the rowdy lower section, the river above the falls flowed through low meadowland from its source in several small lakes. High hills rose toward the southern edge of the central uplands, containing the headwaters of Sisters, Burnthill, Clearwater, and McKiel Brooks.

Ganong and Laskey remained at Spider Lake long enough to make detailed records of this upper region before heading overland by portage

Typical scenic views along the Cains River, July 2012 and 1909

(Bottom: NBM, William Francis Ganong Collection, Image 1987-17-1223-140)

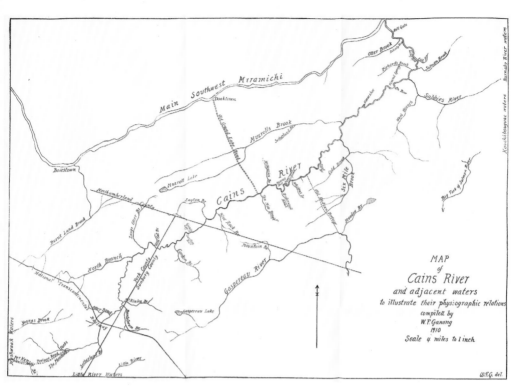

W.F. Ganong's 1909 map of the Cains River and adjacent waters (PANB-MC1799)

roads to Clearwater Brook. They continued down the brook until it met the Southwest Miramichi, followed the main river to Burnthill Brook, and hiked up the Burnthill to the portage road. From there, they crossed to McKiel Brook, following it south to finish the long-distance hike in Juniper with a well-earned respite at Barter's Farm.

Ganong's sense of urgency wouldn't let him rest long, however, and the pair soon left for Fredericton. There, Ganong bid goodbye to Laskey and immediately joined Sam MacDonald for a field trip on the Cains or Ouelamoukt River. Ganong translated the Mi'kmaq name to mean a handsome or fine river, a well-deserved name due to its appealing physiography. The Cains is the longest river totally within the geological zone known as the Maritime Basin, a region of the province consisting of conglomerate and sandstone rock formations. Because of this, the Cains River was ideal for a field trip by canoe since it was free of dangerous rapids and falls.

With supplies replenished, Ganong and MacDonald took their canoe and gear by wagon north along the Nashwaak River to Taymouth. They

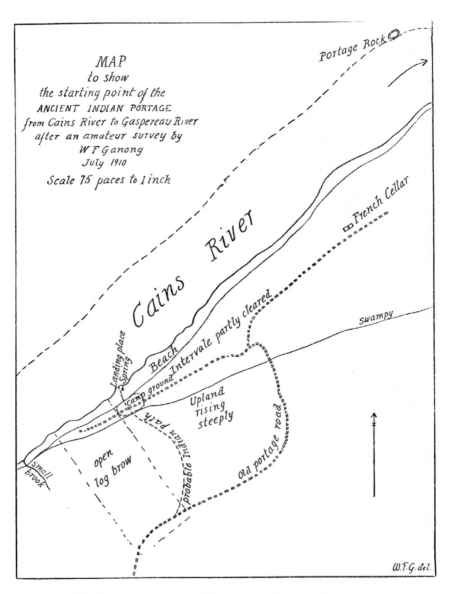

MAP
to show
the starting point of the
ANCIENT INDIAN PORTAGE
from Cains River to Gaspereau River
after an amateur survey by
W F Ganong
July 1910

Scale 75 paces to 1 inch

Portage Rock

Cains River

French Cellar

swampy

Landing place
Spring
Beach
Intervale partly cleared
Camp ground

Upland
rising
steeply

open
log brow

probable Indian path

old portage road

small
brook

W.F.G. del.

W.F. Ganong's 1909 map of the start of the Cains-Gaspereau
Ancient Indian Portage (PANB-MC1799)

climbed overland on the Zionville Portage to the Meadows, crossing from the Saint John to the Miramichi watershed and one of the sources of the Cains River. Ganong's report in the Natural History Society bulletin reveals his complete satisfaction in undertaking this long-anticipated field trip:

> *Accordingly, after long and eagerly looking forward to its study, it was with particular pleasure that I was able in late August and early September last, under good conditions of weather and exceptionally good conditions of water, to descend this river in a canoe from near its source, and observe its physiographic features.*[3]

The headwaters of the Cains lie in a large open basin, which gently slopes from the western region of the province towards the eastern shore along the Northumberland Strait. The two companions worked northeast, pushing through alders, along a dark, peaty stream until it widened enough for paddling. Descending the river, they entered a region that had been scarred by a forest fire a few years earlier, a not uncommon occurrence at the time. Ganong described the regenerating landscape:

> *Here the valley walls soon rise steeply, and the great burnt country is entered which extends for most of the distance to the mouth of the river, though the new growth is developed enough to give the county a rather pleasing park-like aspect in many places.*[4]

While canoeing down the Cains River, Ganong conducted many side excursions. The direction of the Cains changed little through most of its length before it joined the Southwest Miramichi, except below Salmon Brook, where it turned abruptly north. He scouted the brook and the Barnaby River, later making detailed maps. He decided that the Cains had once flowed into the Barnaby, noting "the evidence for such former connection must be chiefly cartographical, but everything I have been able to observe upon the ground is strictly in harmony therewith."[5]

While canoeing, he observed a series of troughs and crests in the landscape, stretching north and south across the path of the river at long intervals much like waves on the ocean. He compared these with similar phenomena he had observed on a larger scale and commented on the geological relationships:

If these troughs and crests actually exist, they are probably minor synclines and anticlines parallel with those larger ones which have given the north coast of New Brunswick its form and have made the Straits of Northumberland and Prince Edward Island.[6]

Beyond his interest in the physiography of the Cains, Ganong was also curious about its early human inhabitants and their use of the river. He knew that the Mi'kmaq and later the French had been forced to travel farther inland upon the arrival of Scottish and Irish settlers. A point of great significance, and one of the prime reasons for his interest, was the exact location of the route they had used to cross overland from the Cains River to the Gaspereau River. In a supplement to his field trip report, Ganong stressed the historical importance of the portage.

One of the most interesting of the features of Cains River and one which will remain of interest to the people of New Brunswick as long as they care for their history at all, is the ancient portage route which connected this river with the Gaspereau, as a link in the most important aboriginal route of travel from the Miramichi to the St. John waters.[7]

He saw it as a crucial factor in understanding the historical development patterns of human settlement in the area.

Their settlement here would be natural for the reason that this river was the great route of travel from the Miramichi to the St. John via the portage to the Gaspereau, a route which was used not only in early Indian and French times but even after the arrival of the Loyalists.[8]

By the time of Ganong's 1909 field trip, the portage was long out of use. It had become overgrown in places reclaimed by the forest, and most of the small settlements had been abandoned. Only a sparse sprinkling of farms remained below the Sabbies River, and his report refers to the movement of younger people to larger towns such as Newcastle and Chatham, or even farther afield to Upper Canada.

Ganong's unwavering determination to discover the precise portage location led him to study survey maps and land grants that indicated the

Portage Rock, Cains River, November 2012

route's existence, followed by interviews with local lumbermen. During this field trip, he carried out a meticulous examination of the site he suspected was the start of the overland trail between watersheds. From his growing knowledge of Mi'kmaq culture, he knew there would have been a camping area with access to good drinking water near the portage. After searching up and down the river, he found a natural spring with a flat, dry area suitable for camping just above it. Ganong and MacDonald followed the age-old practice of camping there, noting that they "camped upon it with a deep feeling of satisfaction in the belief that we had this bond in common with a very long and ancient line of worthy voyageurs."[9] He supported its authenticity in a report to the Natural History Society, writing:

> *All probabilities appear to me to unite in connecting the old Indian path with these places, and I believe there is no doubt that the Indians used the gravel platform as their canoe landing, camped on the dry flat, drew their water from the spring on the shore, and climbed the valley wall by a winding path just behind.*[10]

It was clear to Ganong that he had found the Cains River end of the portage at the most southerly point on the river, where the distance was shortest to the Gaspereau River. His report identifies an easily visible nearby landmark for those coming upriver:

Cold Brook, Cains River, November 2012

*To one ascending the river, the approach to the portage is marked,
in one of the prettiest parts of the whole stream, by the presence, on
the north side of the river, of an immense and conspicuous solitary
sandstone boulder, a flat fragment of ledge which has slipped down
from the low cliffs above and now rests slanting against the bank.
This rock is known universally to all who use the river as Portage
Rock. On its flat surface, by the way, can be traced a crude suggestion
of a human face.*[11]

In the same area, they located an old cellar. Alexander Arbo, a long-time
resident of the Cains River who knew the river intimately, told him that
pieces of pottery, iron axes, and other old relics had been found in the
area. Ganong speculated that they were probably remnants of an Acadian

community from the infamous Great Expulsion or Le Grand Dérangement, when they "had to settle temporarily in retired places beyond reach of their English enemies who were trying to expel them."[12]

Unfortunately the portage itself was overgrown beyond recognition. Ganong and MacDonald hiked to Cold Brook on an old cutting road along the brow of the hill, but the trail beyond the brook was lost. Unsure of the route, Ganong maintained a southwest course as Mr. Arbo had suggested, at one point circumventing a large blowdown of trees that Ganong identified as a result of the Saxby Gale of 1869.

The two explorers stayed on the elevated ridges above the wetlands, arriving at the Gaspereau in the area believed to be the other end of the portage. Using information from correspondence with a Mr. P.H. Welch, a known authority of the Gaspereau River, they hiked half a mile down along the Gaspereau to the outlet of Meadow Brook. From there, Ganong located Portage Island and the other end of the old trail at the most northerly projection of the river, logically placed where the distance between watersheds was shortest. It was little more than a weed-covered sandbar, separated from the mainland by a small bogan or backwater, and easily accessible. Having found the island, he conducted a cursory physiographic study of the surrounding area.

With both ends of the Cains-Gaspereau portage located, Ganong completed his summer fieldwork and was ready to head for home. He returned, however, in 1910 and 1911 to complete his fieldwork on the portage trail itself and to make further maps of the Gaspereau watershed.

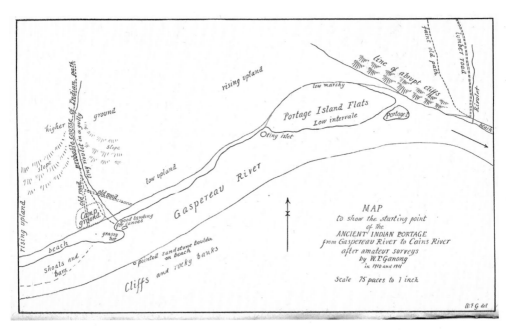

W.F. Ganong's map showing the start of the ancient Indian portage from the
Gaspereau River to the Cains River (PANB-MC1799)

15

Historical Significance

*Cains River Portage, Gaspereau River, and Beaubears
Island, Summer 1910*

For many a year I had gazed longingly upon its somewhat
conventionalized representation upon our maps, with a great
desire to make its personal acquaintance, but it was not until
the summer of 1910 that I was able actually to examine it.

— W.F. GANONG[1]

Ganong felt that the historical significance of the ancient Cains-Gaspereau
portage required more work to finalize the analysis he had begun in 1909.
Before continuing the previous summer's work, he and his friend Samuel
MacDonald took a short trip by wagon from Pleasant Ridge into the headwaters of the Bartholomew River. As usual, Ganong studied the physical
attributes of the river, determining its relationship to the Dungarvan, the
Southwest Miramichi, and the Cains.

After completing this work, MacDonald and Ganong travelled back
up the Southwest Miramichi River to the settlement at Doaktown, where
Ganong met his second companion of the summer, William Laskey. Bidding
goodbye to MacDonald, they were shuttled down the old Grand Lake road
to the bridge spanning the Cains River. From there, the two men hiked
downriver to the starting point of the portage found the year before.
Ganong meticulously retrace the ancient route to the Gaspereau River
and pursued his passion for local history. "In these easy portage routes,"
he noted, "we have an excellent example of the correlation which exists
between physiography and history."[2]

The newly cut portage trail at the Gaspereau end
of the Gaspereau-Cains portage, November 2012

ON OR NEAR THIS SPOT
STARTED THE ANCIENT INDIAN PORTAGE PATH
TO CAINS RIVER.
IT FORMED ONE OF THE IMPORANT LINKS
IN THE CHAIN OF ABORIGINAL ROUTES OF TRAVEL
THROUGH NEW BRUNSWICK,
AND THE PRINCIPAL LINE OF COMMUNICATION
BETWEEN THE MIRAMICHI AND THE LOWER SAINT JOHN.

W.F. Ganong's proposed plaque to mark the ancient
Indian portage from the Gaspereau River to the Cains River

The youthful Laskey showed great patience as Ganong spent several days at the Gaspereau, continuing his fieldwork from the previous summer in greater detail. Ganong had been considering a more careful examination of this particular river for some time. Part of his motivation was his fascination with the First Nations history of the province. In his monograph of 1909, he deemed the ancient portage route that connected the Cains to the Gaspereau to be one of the most historically important and deserving of official recognition. The supplement that he added to his report on the field trip states: "Someday, the important historical sites of the Province will be marked in suitable and permanent fashion by our Historical Societies, and among the first to be fixed in this manner should be the ends of the Cains River–Gaspereau portage."[3]

Ganong had depended on anecdotal information from reliable sources, in particular from Mr. P.H. Welch, to determine the location of the portage. A local guide who had travelled the area extensively, Welch interviewed long-time woodsmen and trappers familiar with the river. All agreed that the location of the portage was just above the Portage Island Ganong had located the previous summer. This gave him added confidence in finding the traditional starting place. Approaching from downriver, he found a gully leading gradually up the slope to the top of the escarpment and was convinced that this was the original trail. He reported they "had little trouble in locating the position of the ancient path, despite the fact that no visible trace of it now remains."[4]

The small swale for the canoe launch, the gully for a pathway, and the flat camping area at the top of the brow all supported his conclusion that

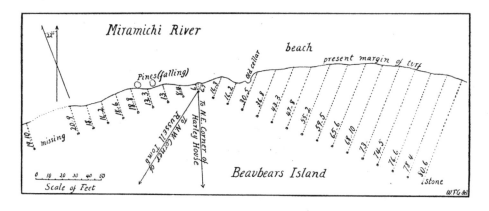

W.F. Ganong's 1910 map of coastal recession on Beaubears Island (PANB-MC1799)

this was the Gaspereau end of the portage.[5] Ganong would later recommend to the Natural History Society that a monument be erected at the site.[6]

With this part of his summer fieldwork completed, Ganong and Laskey hiked along the river to the settlement at Chipman. They returned to Fredericton, where Ganong joined his third companion for the summer. Arthur Pierce, despite his experiences in previous summers, couldn't resist the lure of another field trip with his friend. They travelled a short distance to Boiestown before hiking overland to the upper reaches of the Dungarvan River. Using Braithwaite's hunting trails, they carried equipment and supplies to the Renous Lakes to complete work on this important tributary of the Miramichi River.[7]

For his final 1910 field trip, Ganong wanted to complete the study he and Pierce had begun in 1904 on the recession of New Brunswick's province's eastern shoreline, using Beaubears Island at the confluence of the Northwest and Southwest Miramichi Rivers. With Pierce's help, he located the same post lines in front of the local landmarks of Russell's Tomb and Harley House and measured the distance from each post to the shoreline. They were careful not to look at the previous measurements until the new set was transcribed. When Ganong finally compared the numbers, the dramatic result surprised him. The shoreline had eroded an average of more than half a metre in six years, indicating that it would recede approximately ten metres over a century. Because of the island's sheltered location, he noted, the recession would be conservative compared with shorelines more exposed to the action of the ocean. He suggested this would

The site of Harley House on Beaubears Island
in October 2014, and the house itself, circa 1904.

(Bottom: NBM, William Francis Ganong Collection, Image 987-17-1219-189)

have far-reaching consequences, which "must be taken into account not only in physiographic but also in archaeological studies."[8]

On his map of Beaubears Island, Ganong indicated 1906 as the date of the first set of measurements, but his 1910 report to the Natural History Society clearly states that he made his first measurement in August 1904. "After an interval of exactly six years," he continues, "I was able to measure the offsets by aid of the same methods, the same companion and even the same tape measure."[9]

In September of 2014, I made my way to Beaubears Island with the assistance of Mr. Azade Hache of Nelson, Miramichi. After an hour spent examining the northeastern portion of the island, it was apparent that the fence line Ganong used no longer existed. Tidal erosion and the growth of a pine forest in what was once the front field of Harley House have removed any trace of the posts. All that remains of the house is the outline of the cellar, and Russell's Tomb still stands in the shade of stately pine trees.

16

The Land of Meadows and Water

Gaspereau River and Salmon River, Summer 1911

He always returned well and full of enthusiasm, holding his family breathless with his tales of thrilling experiences in the deep woods.

— SUSAN B. GANONG[1]

In the summer of 1911, Ganong wanted to continue his fieldwork on the Gaspereau River and extend it into the Salmon River. Accompanied by William Laskey, he planned to start with physiographic studies of the Gaspereau and its tributaries, first paddling from its source to the confluence with Salmon River. Ganong felt that the Gaspereau had never been adequately surveyed above the settlement at Cochrane Brook and was intrigued by the fact that it ran through a remarkably little-known wilderness. After this, the pair planned to conduct a careful study of the Salmon River from the headwaters near Harcourt down to Chipman.

They transported their canoe and gear overland from Chipman into the vast heath surrounding Briggs Brook and established a camp at its mouth. Ganong spent time mapping the upper region of the Gaspereau watershed before they launched the canoe in the headwaters of the river at Gaspereau Lake. It was surrounded by large meadows stretching northwest towards Bantalor Brook and the Little River. Ganong described the countryside: "[it] contains some low ridges distinguished by their remarkably fine hemlock trees, while between the ridges lie the swamps, bogs and barrens, everywhere characteristic of this flat sandstone plateau."[2] At first, the river

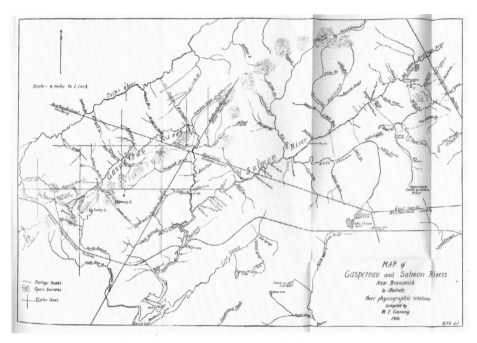

W.F. Ganong's 1912 map of the Gaspereau and Salmon River (PANB-MC1799)

ambled through heath land, where several smaller brooks joined it to form, Ganong explained, what the Maliseet called an obscache, or small stream.

For several miles downstream, the clear brown river ran easterly over a sandy bottom with occasional small rips where there were shallow gravel bars and ledges. Ganong and Laskey hoped to paddle most of the river, but instead found themselves wading beside the canoe as they lined it through low summer water. Fortunately, they had made sure their canoe was "specially prepared by shoe runners, for shallow water, of which we found plenty below Flewelling Brook, though above that point the canoeing was pleasant."[3]

Ganong must have had a sense of déjà vu as they waded past the Cains-Gaspereau portage he had explored the year before. This time, he noted that the Gaspereau above and below the portage coursed eastwards through alternating sandstone ridges until Meadow Brook, where it turned abruptly south before meeting the Salmon River. The river's disposition also changed below the turn at Meadow Brook, taking on postglacial characteristics. Ganong noted that it was "a much newer looking, and apparently much younger, river, with steeper and more cliff-like walls."[4] Along this stretch, the Gaspereau had worn a path through the undulating terrain to a depth

Gaspereau River, September 2014

of thirty metres or more, the slope of the land toward the southeast causing it to wear the southeast banks more aggressively. This abrupt change posed an interesting problem. After hiking up Meadow Brook to investigate the physiographical evidence, Ganong suggested that the original preglacial Gaspereau River must have continued eastward along the brook into the Kouchibouguacis River valley, eventually emptying into the Northumberland Strait.

Just above the bridge over the upper Gaspereau, the river began to flow through extensive intervales until it met the Salmon River at Gaspereau Forks. Ganong and Laskey canoed down the Salmon to Chipman to get provisions for the second phase of the summer field trips. A successful exploration of the Gaspereau River buoyed their spirits as they travelled overland by train to Harcourt Station. At Harcourt Station they hired a wagon for the trip to Smith's Landing on the Salmon River. From there, they poled upriver to the mouth of Hazen Jam Brook, where Ganong measured the elevation above sea level and took compass bearings. As the major river of southeast New Brunswick, the Salmon was well documented on early French maps and in subsequent geological surveys, many done to assess coal deposits. Ganong had a good understanding of the river's

The Gaspereau River just above the Burpee Bridge, July 2012

basic physiography, supplemented by anecdotal information from local residents. Although he did not expect anything unusual, he still wanted to paddle the full length of the river to Grand Lake in order to form scientific opinions based upon his own fieldwork and observations. His report to the Natural History Society confirmed that:

> *Salmon River, as the geological maps well show, lies wholly within the great Carboniferous basin of New Brunswick; and hence nothing is to be anticipated from its geology except the usual jointed gray sandstone of that formation, while its physiography may be expected to harmonize with that of the other rivers in the same region.*[5]

Like the headwaters of the Gaspereau, Cains, and Canaan Rivers, the Salmon River rose from dark peaty waters that formed an elongated still water in the heart of a large barren that dominates the Maritime Basin. Ganong described the uppermost stretch of the river as placid and pretty if rather monotonous, the low banks, "mostly with a border of meadow or alders, backed by birches and poplars, though here and there small groves of princes pine appear on low sandy terraces."[6] The Salmon River was easy canoeing as it flowed easterly through the wide, flat basin before making the first of two sharp turns at a point in the river aptly called the

Oxbow. There, the river almost doubled backed on itself, turning north and becoming swifter as it cut through a slightly elevated terrain, then turning west and regaining its placid slow character.

A few hundred metres from Indian Portage Brook, Ganong and Laskey made a side excursion to try to determine the ancient portage route to the headwaters of the Richibucto River. They found that the portage followed a narrow sandstone ridge with the land sloping west to the Salmon River and east to the Richibucto. Ganong observed that the wide land basin between was no more than thirty metres above sea level, even at its highest point by the Oxbow. He speculated that it would not take a huge geological change to allow seawater to flood inland from the Northumberland Strait, completely changing the province's geography. He envisioned the whole region underwater in preglacial times, from the mouth of the Salmon to the Bay of Fundy, saying:

> *The origin of this basin is plain enough. It lies exactly in the line of that great trough, occupied by the Richibucto and Salmon Rivers, which almost converts the part of New Brunswick southeast of it into a separate island; for it would require a depression of not much over 100 feet, as the railway levels show, to fill this trough with salt water all the way from Richibucto Harbour to Saint John Harbour.*[7]

Back on the Salmon River, Ganong and Laskey paddled easily through long stretches of calm water interspersed with short sections of shallow rips. The river became faster at Lake Brook, with more frequent small rapids as it cut through a series of undulating ridges. One of the main tributaries of the river, the brook has its source in two lakes located in the large central barren dominating the region. Locals claimed that the upper lake was poisonous to fish, recounting how large numbers were sometimes found dead in the water and on the shore. Since Ganong believed in a scientific explanation for every natural occurrence, he theorized that "at times in these shallow and fish-infested lakes, the supply of dissolved oxygen, essential to the support of fish life, falls for some reason below the normal, causing the death of the weaker individuals."[8] Later, he was pleased to find his theory substantiated in a 1912 article on oxygen deficiency in lakes, published in German in *Deutsche Landwirtschaftliche Presse*.[9]

At the confluence of the Salmon and Gaspereau Rivers, Ganong and Laskey pulled their canoe onto the shore, their summer field trips finished.

The beauty and tranquility of the Salmon River, June 2012

Exploring the river was of little interest beyond this point since it flowed through well-settled farmland to Grand Lake.

Ganong returned to Salmon River with Leonard Smith of Grangeville, Kent County, in the summer of 1913. From Chipman, they boarded the eastbound train and were dropped off close enough to carry the canoe and their gear to Upper Lake. Ganong conducted research around the headwaters of Lake Stream, before he and Smith canoed down the Salmon River to Chipman. Another train trip eastward to the headwaters of Coal Creek followed. These were just two of many short trips that Ganong made to complete his physiographic studies of the region.

17

The Land of Canaan

Bouctouche to the Canaan River, Summer 1912

> My trip along the main river from near Canaan Station to
> the Saint John was made in company with my brother Mr.
> W.K. Ganong. It was part of a canoe journey from Baie Verte
> to Fredericton via the sea coast, the Buctouche (sic) River
> (to the head of tide), the Washademoak and the Saint John,
> — a route and method little used in our day though having,
> I believe, abundant precedents in former times.
>
> — W.F. Ganong[1]

August 1912 saw Ganong once again exploring the southeastern region
of the province, this time in the company of his younger brother Walter.
They planned an ambitious trip, studying the wetlands at the headwaters
of the Bouctouche and Canaan Rivers and continuing down the Canaan
River. The brothers wanted to locate and document another important
portage, this time the ancient Bouctouche-Washademoak route that the
Mi'kmaq peoples had used to travel from the Northumberland Strait to
the Saint John River watershed. The "Maliseet Indians of the River Saint
John doubtless made use of this route at times," Ganong explained in his
report. "The Micmac's of Prince Edward Island used to come regularly
by this route to hunt on the Upper Canaan in autumn and winter, and
they had an important camp ground on the Millstream, the MacDonald
Brook of our map."[2]

First, though, Ganong wanted to study the peculiar tides on the eastern
shore at Bouctouche. Several years earlier, he found information stating that
the tides in that harbour were governed by the winds blowing on shore with

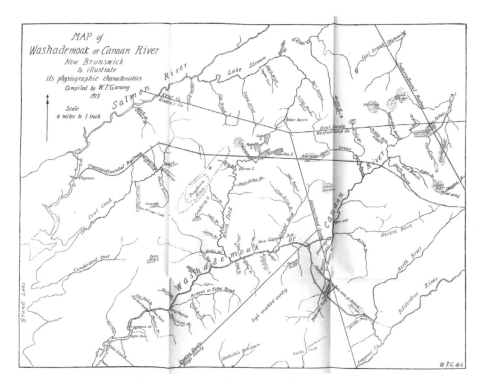

W.F. Ganong's 1910 map of the Washademoak or Canaan River (PANB-MC1799)

great energy, forcing the tides to rise and fall once in every twenty-four hours rather than the normal twelve-hour cycle. Locals believed this was caused not by wind but by sand islands at the mouth of the harbour hindering the escape of water from the river and estuary. Ganong was not convinced.

Heading west from the settlement at Bouctouche, the brothers canoed upriver to study the prolonged tide cycle. They camped at the head of the tide near Coates Mill and observed the phenomenon on the morning of July 29, 1912. In contrast to both of the theories he'd heard, Ganong concluded that the unusual tides were the result either of the way in which the waters met after passing around Prince Edward Island, or of an unexplained astronomical influence.

The two men then made their way up the Bouctouche River and a smaller tributary until they found an overgrown path that Ganong hoped was the traditional Bouctouche-Canaan portage route. They successfully carried their canoe and gear over the watershed divide to the easternmost part of the Canaan headwaters. Ganong later learned that the route they had followed was a road built years before to haul stone from Bouctouche Harbour for construction of the Inter-Colonial Railway.

Starting in a large bog, the Canaan River was originally known by the Mi'kmaq as the Washademoak, but the Loyalist settlers of New Canaan, Connecticut, renamed it for the home they had left behind. Similar to the Salmon River and others in the region, the waters of the Canaan and its seventeen tributaries ran dark brown from the tannic acid in the bogs and barrens at its source. One of the principal tributaries of the lower Saint John River, its headwater meadows extended south to the hills of the southern highlands and north beyond the Salmon River. It was an area that had long intrigued Ganong.

Ganong made several side excursions into the meadows to verify points of interest and take elevation measurements and temperature readings. Then, he and Walter slipped their canoe into the Canaan River to paddle west through the low, undulating country. Moving away from the barren, the river became more clearly defined and its bed changed to gravel and sandstone as they went westward toward Washademoak Lake. As they descended the river, Ganong noted the banks gradually rose further above the water, while small boulders and ledges formed a series of rips. When they reached the train bridge spanning the river, just above the Lower North Branch Canaan, Ganong noted that: "The great height of this bridge, (eighty feet above the stream, which is here about 150 feet above the sea), shows that the general elevation of the country is higher above the river than one would suspect."[3]

The water level was low, forcing the brothers to haul their canoe and equipment over the shoals for several miles. Just below the Petitcodiac Road bridge, Ganong noted an unusual granite outcrop standing out from the sandstone that dominated the region's geology. Continuing downriver, they entered the broad, open countryside and gently rolling hills of New Canaan. Ganong was particularly impressed by the uniform contours of the landscape "and especially by the regularity of the convex up-roll of the grassy and bushy banks to the terrace of equal uniformity of height, some fifteen feet above the river."[4]

Ganong was excited to find the portage between the Washademoak (Canaan) and the Petitcodiac located just above the bridge spanning the river at New Canaan. He believed this was "one of the most important of all the early portage paths in New Brunswick, for it lay on the route

Upper Canaan River, July 2012

of the old French and Indian line of travel between the Chignecto region and Quebec."[5]

True to form, Ganong inspected every tributary of the river, following along the banks and recording noteworthy features. He noted that the landscape changed just beyond the North Fork tributary, becoming similar to the undulating country along the Cains and Salmon Rivers. The tributary started almost ninety-two metres above sea level at Snowshoe Lake then dropped quickly, knifing through an unusual ledge in the sandstone before joining the Canaan. This feature intrigued Ganong, and he would later determine its importance while interviewing Chief James Paul of the St. Mary's First Nation about geographical names.

He told me, however, that a curious ledge near the mouth of the North Fork Stream gave origin to the Indian name of that stream, Sagunik, which word, he said, means a gill of a fish, the rock having that appearance. He refers here of course, to one of the exposures of these laminated argillites.[6]

The only rapids on the entire river were below Riders Brook. This was the only section difficult to navigate by canoe. After that, the Canaan flowed slowly and smoothly to Washademoak Lake through channels formed by small sandstone islands.

In his report to the Natural History Society, Ganong explained the placid character of the Canaan River:

Washademoak Lake, August 2011

> *A striking feature of the Washademoak River is the smallness of*
> *its drop from the great basin at Nevers Brook and especially from*
> *the head of the "canal" near Alward Brook down to tidewater*
> *at Coles Island, the drop, indeed being smaller than that of any*
> *equal length of river known to me in New Brunswick outside of*
> *the estuarine lower Saint John.*[7]

The brothers canoed from the Washademoak into the Saint John River just below the Cambridge Narrows and paddled upriver to Fredericton, ending the 1912 summer field trip.

SUNDRY ITEMS

Thoughts on Natural Curiosities

On Reported Occurrences of the Panther
(Felis Concolor) in New Brunswick[1]

Here, beside a portage road, are partridge feathers in the road;
some of the cat tribe has seized its prey here....

The idea for this item occurred to Ganong when he read the following
article about a panther (felis concolor) sighting by Dr. Van Buren Thorne
and his father. It paints a picture of a sudden encounter with the rare
panther or cougar, when they were hunting in the Canaan woods:

> *A moment later there was a great confused cracking of branches a*
> *hundred yards away to the left. It sounded like a moose on the run.*
> *The sounds became plainer. The animal was evidently approaching.*
> *There was a pause, followed by a growling sound and more stealthy*
> *approach. The animal crept to within twenty feet, then crouched*
> *in the underbrush and growled steadily. A patch of the creatures*
> *tawny hide showed for a moment in an opening of the underbrush.*
> *The animal's identity was no longer a mystery — it was a panther.*
> *There was not time to speculate then to what strange mischance had*
> *led an animal of this species, hitherto unknown in these regions, to*
> *invade the Canaan woods. It was time for action. The creature was*
> *lashing itself into a perfect gale of fury and growling ominously. As*
> *he crouched again to spring I fired blindly where the ferns quivered.*
> *His growling ceased and he forbore to spring. Instead, he turned and*
> *leaped haltingly and lamely away. The blood on the leaves showed*
> *that he was wounded, but pursuit, owing to the dense nature of the*
> *woods at this point, was futile.*

Intrigued by the story, Ganong interviewed Dr. Thorne and did some further research to see if he could substantiate the sighting. He wrote that the doctor held firm that he had seen a panther, despite all arguments to the contrary. Ganong's report states that the *Saint John Gazette* interviewed Boaz Corey of Canaan, who claimed to have trapped a monster Indian Devil, the local name for a panther. The article stated that it appeared to have been recently wounded and speculated that it was the same animal seen by Thorne. Unfortunately, it turned out that the cat trapped by Corey was a lynx, so the cat Thorne had shot was either not a panther or was still at large. Ganong wrote of the conundrum: "The Indian Devil is that animal which, when seen, is never believed to have been seen by anybody but the person who saw it."

Ganong's research found no historical record of panther sightings in the province. In his report, he concluded that Thorne had been mistaken about the cat. The description of the animal's behaviour seemed to indicate that it was a lynx, a wild cat known to show little fear of man, but not a cougar, which by nature is stealthy, silent, and usually shy of humans. On January 6, 1903, Ganong presented his report to the Natural History Society, summarizing: "We are brought to the conclusion that there is not a solitary authentic record, or any other authentic evidence, of either the present or former occurrence of the panther within the limits of New Brunswick."

New Brunswick Animals and the Animal Romancers[2]

The charm of the study to the man of science is the triumph of demonstrating the truth. He makes this his sole standard, as it is his sole reward.

For Ganong, scientifically proven information was essential for any presentation or publication about the natural world. This led to his profound dislike of a growing practice among fiction writers to anthropomorphize animal behaviour. Ganong believed they were misleading readers by presenting these animals with human feelings, behaviours, and thought processes. He also chastised book reviewers who wrote glowing reviews of the stories without any scientific background. His opinions are clear in 1905:

The last quarter of a century has seen a remarkable development in that form of literature which consists of charming popular writings about animals and their doings not as they are, but as people like to think they are. [These writers] have given their imaginations full play, thus producing fascinating works of fiction disguised as natural history. It is however this disguise which constitutes the ground of criticism against these works.

He specifically criticized the animal stories of American cleric William Long and acclaimed New Brunswick writer Sir Charles G.D. Roberts. Since Roberts was married to a cousin of Ganong's wife, this must have made for some interesting dinner conversations. William Long, a church minister, found himself at the centre of this controversy through his stories about animal parents teaching behaviours to their young. Despite the wide audience for Long's stories, Ganong felt they lacked scientific rigour and clearly contradicted scientific facts, saying they "seem to me to show that he has little idea of the nature of evidence or of logical proof, and that he possesses neither the temperament nor the training." In a letter to Ganong, Long politely suggests Ganong's reaction is based on personal experience, not science:

As for the criticism itself, it seems to me honest and to be fairly free from that unscientific venom which has characterized one or two recent criticisms from professed scientific people. In the interest of truth, I am glad you wrote it, if you felt that way; but I have an idea that sooner or later you will regret having published it. Summed up, your whole criticism is this: my observations are contrary to your experience, therefore you disbelieve them.

Ganong agreed that Long's intentions were good but suggested that emotion swayed his written interpretations of animal behaviour. Long replied that he was simply repeating information provided by wildlife experts. He claimed that Ganong's own wilderness companion, Mauran Furbish, had told him about a kingfisher killing a fish, dropping it into a shallow pond, and using it to teach its chicks how to catch a live fish. When Ganong checked the story with Furbish, his friend admitted only to telling Long about a dead Gaspereau found near the edge of a lake, noting that Long had taken literary liberties with the story.

Ganong was even more disparaging of Roberts, suggesting that he was deliberately misleading the public by pretending first-hand knowledge of wild animals in their natural setting. It was acceptable to use information accumulated from sources, he said, but not without giving appropriate credit. Furthermore, Ganong asserted that Roberts had not had the opportunity or time while growing up in Douglas (near Fredericton) to study wild animals such as moose, caribou, bear, and lynx in their natural surroundings. Instead, he suggested:

> *His knowledge of these animals must have been gained mostly in the public libraries, museums and menageries of New York City, and his interpretations of their psychology, upon which latterly he lays some stress, can have little basis other than in his own imagination.*

Ganong wrote that Roberts should acknowledge in the preface to his books that they were "not based upon personal observation of their subjects, but are as accurate as he can make them from other sources of information." In this item for the Natural History Society bulletin, he called the stories "remarkable imaginative works," but decried the tendency of new nature writers to present unproven facts and imagination as legitimate fact.

On Vegetable, or Burr, Balls from Little Kedron Lake[3]

Unexplained curiosities fascinated Ganong, leading him to report on some rather unusual topics related to natural phenomenon. On a visit to Fredericton, he had been shown a specimen of an unusual-looking ball of dense vegetable matter that was more than ten centimetres in diameter. It had been found on the shores of Little Kedron Lake. A lack of information about the ball's nature and formation was enough to inspire the ever-curious naturalist to investigate. Ganong's research led him to Wellington Davis of Brockway, York County, who sent him a similar specimen to the one he had seen, along with a note:

> *I cannot tell you very much about it. It is found in the north end of the Little Kedron Lake in a small cove. No wind can strike the cove but from the southeast. It is surrounded with fir and spruce, which hang over the water. The bottom is clear sand. The spills drop from the fir*

W.F. Ganong's photo of Little Kedron Lake burr ball in comparison
with that of Flint or Sandy Pond in Massachusetts

*and spruce and lie at the bottom. Then the water washing them from
side to side forms the ball. These balls can be found in no other place
in the Little Kedron Lake, nor in Big Kedron Lake. . . . Sometimes
we have found them from six to eight inches through.*

Ganong also corresponded with other botanists about the strange spheres,
receiving little additional information. However, he did find a description of the phenomenon in the ninth chapter of Henry David Thoreau's
Walden and reports of the discovery of similar formations at Sandy Pond
in Lincoln, Massachusetts. Ganong eventually formulated the following
assumption about the nature and formation of the burr balls:

*They are nothing more than the result of the rolling about of vege-
table fragments on hard sandy bottoms by the action of the underwater parts of waves. . . . The material collects first in ripple marks,
there becoming somewhat matted together in short loose cylinders;
as these enlarge they are rolled out and over the bottom, where,
gathering other material, they gradually become larger, rounder,
and more compact. It is not improbable that micro-organisms
develop within them, and by forming zoogolea or other glutinous
matter, help to fasten them together.*

It seems that Ganong derived much satisfaction from solving nature's riddles, even the simplest ones, such as the effect of wave motion, or the formation of a burr ball, a testament to his inquisitive mind and need for scientific explanations.

On the Limits of the Great Fire of Miramichi of 1825[4]

When Ganong began his forays into the headwaters of the Miramichi watershed, seventy-five years had passed since the Great Fire. Yet its consequences were still evident in the natural and human history of the area. The process of natural reforestation after a fire interested Ganong, but he found the existing information about the massive conflagration too unreliable to be useful. The written accounts he found all differed on the extent of the fire and the communities affected. Estimates of the area burned varied by thousands of acres, while some reports stated that entire settlements were destroyed and others that they were spared the wrath of the fire.

One undisputed fact was the date of the fire on October 7, 1825, during an unusually prolonged dry period. Whipped by hurricane-force winds, several small, unrelated forest fires joined to form a formidable blaze throughout the entire Miramichi River basin. "At Douglastown, scarcely any kind of property escaped the ravage of the fire. The Town of Newcastle with all the surrounding settlements became a total waste," eyewitness Alexander Rankin reported in an account published a mere four days later. "Four miles through the interior," he noted, "the greatest desolation took place."

Ganong considered that the best-known account of the fire was written in 1832 by W.H. (Robert) Cooney in his *Compendious History of the Northern Part of the Province of New Brunswick, and of the District of Gaspe in Lower Canada*. Situating himself in Newcastle at the mouth of the Miramichi, Cooney set the scene by noting the unseasonable summer heat and a drought that had continued well into the autumn. Following is his dramatic description of the day of the fire:

> *About 12 o'clock, a pale sickly mist, lightly tinged with purple, emerged from the forest, and settled over it. This cloud soon retreated before a large dark one, which occupying its place, wrapt*

the firmament in a pall of vapour. This incumbrance, retaining its position, till about three o'clock, the heat became tormentingly sultry. There was not a single breath of air. The temperature was overloaded; — an irresistible lassitude seized the people; and a stupefying dullness seemed to pervade every place but the woods which now trembled, and rustled, and shook, with an incessant and thrilling noise of explosions rapidly following each other, and mingling their reports with a discordant variety of loud and boisterous sounds. At this time, the whole country appeared to be encircled by a Fiery Zone.

Ganong also unearthed accounts written years later, some of which included even the Tobique watershed in the limits of the fire. He decided to focus his own research on a series of interviews with old-time woodsmen. They had worked along the various tributaries of the Miramichi and knew the difference between trees that had grown since the fire and the older stands. One of the leading lumbermen of the region, Mr. E. Hutchison of Douglastown, was confident that many of the accounts were exaggerated. He based his opinion of the fire's extent on the difference in the age of trees cut inside and outside the burned areas, pointing out to Ganong that "the basin of the Renous, Dungarvan and Bartholomew Rivers have all produced immense quantities of logs much older than could have grown since the great fire."

The information Ganong gathered indicated that the fire had begun with a patchwork of localized forest fires scattered in a triangular region, extending from close to Fredericton and across the Miramichi watershed to the province's eastern shore. In the days before October 7, strong, warm winds spread these unrelated fires, producing aggressive infernos that encompassed larger and larger areas. This, Ganong suggested, explained why some communities and not others were spared, and why the Cains River and Gaspereau River watersheds were extensively burned, while the Renous, Dungarvan, and Bartholomew River watersheds remained relatively untouched. Thanks to local first-hand knowledge, Ganong was able to make a satisfactory map of the extent of the Great Fire of Miramichi.

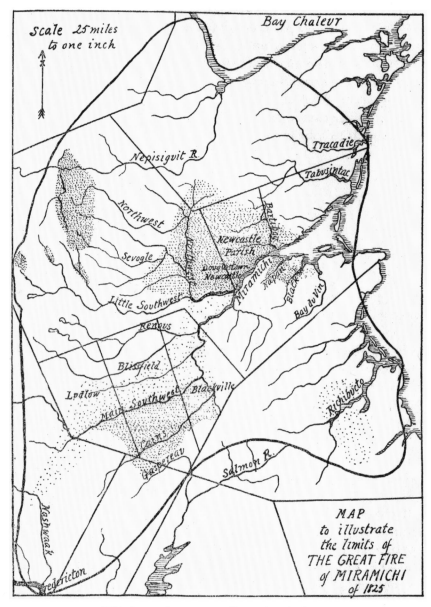

Within the map:

Scale 25 miles
to one inch

Bay Chaleur

Nepisiguit R.

Tracadie

Tabusintac

Northwest

Sevogle

Newcastle
Parish

Bartibog

Little Southwest

Douglastown
Newcastle

Miramichi

Napan

Black

Bay du Vin

Renous

Blissfield

Ludlow

Main Southwest

Blackville

Richibucto

Cains

Gaspereau

Salmon R.

MAP
to illustrate
the limits of
THE GREAT FIRE
of MIRAMICHI
of 1825

Nashwaak

Fredericton

W.F. Ganong's 1905 map illustrating the limits
of the Great Fire of Miramichi of 1825 (PANB-MC1799)

The Fact Basis of the Fire (or Phantom) Ship of the Bay of Chaleur[5]

While exploring the Acadian Peninsula in 1905, Ganong had the opportunity to investigate the Phantom Ship of the Bay of Chaleur. At first he was skeptical of the fanciful tale, but he began to suspect that a natural phenomenon manifested itself as fire on the bay and was mistakenly identified as a ghost vessel.

Ganong interviewed several fisherman and sea captains, learning that the phenomenon was not associated with any particular season or location on the bay. They also told him that it looked like a column of fire on the water, and its occurrence was a precursor to a storm. Ganong had some reservations about their accounts, later reporting:

> *Of course I have sifted all testimony to the best of my ability, eliminating all exaggerations and embellishments, whether these be due to the habit of all humanity to make a story big and good as possible, or to the common tendency to gull an impressionable stranger.*

He developed a theory about the phenomenon. To support it, he solicited opinion from experts in climatology and reviewed published research on the topic. He concluded that the phantom ship was, in fact, St. Elmo's fire, an electrical discharge caused by a build-up of static electricity and usually associated with a storm. Ganong concluded that the phantom ship phenomenon required further study.

On the Occurrence of the Wolf in New Brunswick[6]

Following his report to the Natural History Society about the credibility of panther sightings in New Brunswick, Ganong decided to analyze occurrences of the grey wolf (*Canis occidentalis*). He believed that the only conclusive evidence of wolves, if they existed in the province, would come from four sources: historical accounts, studies by naturalists, government bounty records, and the testimony of trappers.

With respect to historical records, Ganong reported that there were no references to wolves in either Marc Lescarbot's 1609 inventory of animals in Acadia in his *Histoire de la Nouvelle-France* or in Nicolas Deny's account of his experiences in Acadia between 1631 and 1670, in which he wrote about the flora and fauna of Acadia. Furthermore, Ganong stated that the account by John Gyles of his captivity with the Maliseet from 1689 to 1695 mentions seeing moose, bear, caribou, and beaver, but makes no mention of wolf.[7] Ganong did find wolves recorded in a list of furs exported through the port of Saint John between 1764 and 1774. A century later, though, an 1894 article he found in the American Museum of Natural History bulletin stated definitively that the grey wolf had been extinct in New Brunswick for many years and cited a local authority, who was an expert collector of animals and worked in the Tobique woods.

Although the number of early sightings within the province was small, Ganong found evidence that there had been wolves. In 1792, the Legislature of New Brunswick had even acted to protect domestic livestock, establishing a bounty. In his article, Ganong quoted the reasoning in the legislation: "Whereas many losses have been suffered by sundry Inhabitants of this Province from the destruction of their Sheep by Wolves."

According to Ganong, the presence of wolves in the province's wood-lands and near settlements was much better documented between the years 1841 and 1864. All the witnesses indicated that they or acquaintances had heard the howling of wolves throughout the night. One particularly credible witness was Dr. Abraham Gesner, who was conducting a geological survey of the province during the winter of 1841 to 1842. He reported hearing wolves howling nightly on the Eel River in Carleton County and saw a pack of eleven wolves on Eel River Lake. Others told of finding wolf tracks in the snow when they were hunting.

Throughout the latter part of the century, New Brunswick newspapers reported the reappearance of the wolf, but most of the articles lacked real evidence. Naturalists of the period speculated that the wolves followed the migration of whitetail deer into the province, and as the deer popu-lation fluctuated, so did that of its primary predator. However, this was speculation based on general scientific principles.

Ganong placed most of his confidence in the testimony of woodsmen and professional guides, such as Arthur Pringle of Stanley, but even they provided conflicting information, and some completely denied there were wolves in the province:

> *Mr. Henry Braithwaite, the acknowledged leader of all New Brunswick guides and trappers, whose territory lies in the very wildest part of the Province writes me, — As you are well aware I have followed hunting for over fifty years. I have never seen a track nor have I heard a wolf.*

On the other hand, information from Mr. Welch of Fulton Brook, Queens County, proved the animals' presence — if he could be believed. Welch told Ganong that he had seen wolves and had actually shot one. He also said he had come across tracks of a wolf pack hunting down a caribou on the Snowshoe Barren between Canaan and Lake Stream and had seen one not far from his home as recently as 1901.

Never one to miss an opportunity, Ganong used his report to the society to reinforce his arguments against the "Animal Romancers." He quoted from a June 1906 article in *Everybody's Magazine* in which Theodore Roosevelt, the president of the United States, condemned one of Sir Charles G. D. Roberts's stories dealing with wolves and lynxes. According to Ganong, the president stated that it was absurd and impossible for a lynx to win a fight against eight wolves and went on to caution Roberts to be careful mixing imagination with truth. Roberts defended his position, saying he was thoroughly familiar with the habits of wolves and his writings were based on long, careful observation. Ganong refuted this claim, saying that wolves had all but disappeared from New Brunswick by 1867. Mr. Roberts had been born in 1860, so he could not be an expert or in a position to write authoritatively about wolves.

Ganong concluded his report by stating that the occurrence of wolves was rare in New Brunswick during the 1600s, but the numbers slowly increased until the mid-1700s and were abundant by the 1840s. However, their numbers diminished again, probably due to a decrease in the deer population, and they were practically extirpated in the province by 1867, except for a few remaining in the Salmon River area of Kent County.

provided conflicting information, and some completely denied there were wolves in the province:

> *Mr. Henry Braithwaite, the acknowledged leader of all New Brunswick guides and trappers, whose territory lies in the very wildest part of the Province writes me, — As you are well aware I have followed hunting for over fifty years. I have never seen a track nor have I heard a wolf.*

On the other hand, information from Mr. Welch of Fulton Brook, Queens County, proved the animals' presence — if he could be believed. Welch told Ganong that he had seen wolves and had actually shot one. He also said he had come across tracks of a wolf pack hunting down a caribou on the Snowshoe Barren between Canaan and Lake Stream and had seen one not far from his home as recently as 1901.

Never one to miss an opportunity, Ganong used his report to the society to reinforce his arguments against the "Animal Romancers." He quoted from a June 1906 article in *Everybody's Magazine* in which Theodore Roosevelt, the president of the United States, condemned one of Sir Charles G. D. Roberts's stories dealing with wolves and lynxes. According to Ganong, the president stated that it was absurd and impossible for a lynx to win a fight against eight wolves and went on to caution Roberts to be careful mixing imagination with truth. Roberts defended his position, saying he was thoroughly familiar with the habits of wolves and his writings were based on long, careful observation. Ganong refuted this claim, saying that wolves had all but disappeared from New Brunswick by 1867. Mr. Roberts had been born in 1860, so he could not be an expert or in a position to write authoritatively about wolves.

Ganong concluded his report by stating that the occurrence of wolves was rare in New Brunswick during the 1600s, but the numbers slowly increased until the mid-1700s and were abundant by the 1840s. However, their numbers diminished again, probably due to a decrease in the deer

Acknowledgements

Several individuals deserve my gratitude for their support and friendship throughout this project: Gary Tozer of Miramichi City, Terry Gallant of Turtle Creek, Rod O'Connell of Nigadoo, John Toulman of Minto, Elmo MacDonald of Fredericton Junction, Brian Mercier of Miramichi City, Karl Branch of Bathurst, and Azade Hache of Nelson. Last but not least, I would like to thank Armand Paul, a descendant of the Ganong family, for his guidance and support in the editing of the manuscript.

This book would not have been possible without the support and understanding of the love of my life, Marlaine Roberts, and our children Sarah, Eammon, and Liam.

APPENDIX A
W.F. Ganong's Field Trips

1880 Musquash River (Clinch Stream): located west of Saint John and flowing into the Bay of Fundy.

1881 St. Croix River

1882 St. Croix River

1883 Saint John River, Charlotte County islands and rivers, and Bocabec: Bocabec is located to the northeast of Saint Andrews.

1884 Moose Island, Grand Manan: Moose Island is in the Bay of Fundy near Blacks Harbour.

1885 Squatook, Madawaska River, Frye Island, Chamcook: Squatook Lakes and mountain are located to the east of Lake Temiscouata in Gaspé, Quebec, and form the headwaters of the Madawaska River. Frye is an island in the Bay of Fundy located southeast of Back Bay. Chamcook is a mountain and lake located near Saint Andrews.

1886 Schoodic Lake, Frye Island: Schoodic is currently known as the Chiputneticook chain of lakes that includes East Grand Lake, Spednic, and Palfrey.

1887 Chepedneak: also known as Chiputneticook.

1888 Grand Manan

1889 Woolastook: most likely the Saint John River above Fredericton.

1890 Miramichi River: Main Southwest Miramichi below Boiestown.

1891 Lower Saint John River, Pocologan: Pocologan is a seaside community on the Bay of Fundy.

1892 Oceragabena (Lake Temiscouta)

1893 Attending university in Munich.

1894 Attending university in Munich.

1895 Magaguadavic River, Lepreau River

1896 Restigouche River, Peat Bog Trip: Field trip to a peat bog in Charlotte County.

1897 Lepreau River

1898 Nepisiguit River — Tobique River

1899 Tobique River — Nepisiguit River

1900   Negoot (Tobique River – Riley Brook), Magaguadavic, and Digdeguash Rivers: Negoot is currently the series of lakes forming the headwaters of the Right-Hand Branch of the Tobique River. They include, Long, Trousers, and Island Lakes.

1901   Tuadook (Tobique River to Miramichi Watershed): Tuadook Lake is located on the South Branch of the Little Southwest Miramichi River.

1902   Adder Lake Stream, Southeast and Main Upsalquitch River: Adder Lake Stream is a tributary of the Tobique River located in the central highlands of New Brunswick. The Southeast and Main Upsalquitch is part of the Restigouche River watershed.

1903   Oromocto River, Tobique River to Miramichi River: In particular the Oromocto Lake and North Branch Oromocto River. Little Tobique River to Nepisiguit River with emphasis on the South Branch Nepisiguit and portage to Northwest Miramichi River.

1904   Negoot Lakes, Tuadook (Tobique) River, Renous River: Renous is a tributary of the Main Southwest Miramichi River.

1905   Tobique River to Bathurst, Tracadie River, Pokemouche River, Miscou Island.

1906   Guagus, North Branch North Pole, Kagoot (Big Bald Mountain), Sevogle River, Tabusintac River: Guagus River is a tributary of Tobique River, the North Pole Stream is a tributary of the Little Southwest Miramichi, Kagoot is currently known as Big Bald Mountain, Sevogle is a tributary of the Northwest Miramichi River.

1907   Saint John River, Tobique River

1908   Upper Main Southwest Miramichi River, Wapske to Gulguac, Burnt Hill, Clearwater Stream to Sisters, Lower Miramichi: Wapske is a tributary of the Tobique River; Burnt Hill, Clearwater, and Sisters are tributaries of the Main Southwest Miramichi River.

1909   Rocky Brook to Gulguac, Cains River: Rocky Brook and Cains River are tributaries of the Main Southwest Miramichi.

1910   Bartholomew River, Cains River to Gaspereau Portage, Dungarvan River, Nashwaak River: The Bartholomew is a tributary of the Main Southwest Miramichi River, the Gaspereau is a tributary of the Salmon River that flows into Grand Lake, the Dungarvan is a tributary of the Renous River, and the Nashwaak is a tributary of the Saint John River.

1911   Chemmipic to Obaeache (Harcourt to Grand Lake): Chemmipic is the aboriginal name for the Gaspereau River; Obaeache is the aboriginal name for the Salmon River that starts in Kent County and flows into Grand Lake.

1912   Nova Scotia (following Champlain), Green River and Grand River, North Shore to Baie Verte to Bouctouche: Green and Grand Rivers are tributaries of the Saint John River; Baie Verte is near Port Elgin.

1913   Petitcodiac to Canaan Portage, Magaguadavic River, Lake Stream, Coal Creek, North Forks Canaan: Lake Stream, Coal Creek, and North Forks Canaan are all tributaries of the Canaan River.

1914   Pollett River, Petitcodiac River, Kennebecasis River, Nepisiguit River, Miramichi River, Bathurst, Boiestown: the Pollett River is a tributary of the Petitcodiac River.

1915   Shogomoc River, Pokiok River, Magaguadavic River, Digdeguash River, Tetagouche River, Jacquet River, Nepisiguit River, Gordon Brook, Portage River: Shogomoc (Stream) River and Pokiok (Stream) River are tributaries of the Saint John River, Gordon Brook is a tributary of the Nepisiguit River, and Portage River is a tributary of the Northwest Miramichi River.

1916   Long Lake, New River, Piskehegan River, Chiputneticook Lakes to Madawamkeetook, Seepnakik Pikakatik (S.B. Oromocto – Musquash): Long Lake can be either East or West Long Lake in the Lepreau watershed, Piskahegan River is a tributary of the Magaguadavic River, Madawamkeetook is Maliseet for the Eel River in York County.

1917 Shin Creek, Scoodic Lakes, Clinch Stream (West. Branch. Musquash), Woolastook (Saint John River) to Grand Lake: Shin Creek is a tributary of the South Branch Oromocto River.

1918 Hammond River, Wolves Islands, Kings to Albert County by auto, Kennepak (Kennebecasis River to Saint John): Hammond River is a tributary of the Kennebecasis River, the Wolves are a group of small rocky islands located in the Bay of Fundy, approximately twelve kilometres south of Blacks Harbour.

1919 Upper Saint John Branches

1919-29 Various auto trips in New Brunswick and Gaspé, Quebec.

APPENDIX B

W.F. Ganong's Published Notes on the Natural History and Physiography of New Brunswick

1885-1896

"The Zoology of the Invertebrate Animals of Passamaquoddy Bay." *Bulletin of the Natural History Society of New Brunswick* [hereafter *Bulletin of the NHS*] 4 (1885): 87-97.

"The Marine Mollusca of New Brunswick." *Bulletin of the NHS* 6 (1887): 17-61.

"The Cray-fish in New Brunswick." *Bulletin of the NHS* 6 (1887): 74-75.

"The Echinodermata of New Brunswick." *Bulletin of the NHS* 7 (1888): 12-68.

"The Economic Mollusca of Acadia." *Bulletin of the NHS* 8 (1889): 3-116.

"An Outline of Phytobiology." *Bulletin of the NHS* 9 (1896): 3-15.

1896-1917 (Notes 1 to 138)

Note 1: "Upon Remarkable Sounds, Like Gun Reports, Heard Upon our Southern Coast." *Bulletin of the NHS* 9 (1896): 40-42.

Note 2: "The Outlet-Delta of Lake Utopia." *Bulletin of the NHS* 9 (1896): 43-47.

Note 3: "Upon Temperature-Measurements with the Thermophone in Clear Lake, Lepreau." *Bulletin of the NHS* 9 (1896): 47-52.

Note 4: "On the Color of the Water in New Brunswick Rivers." *Bulletin of the NHS* 16 (1898): 44-45.

Note 5: "On the Heights of New Brunswick Hills." *Bulletin of the NHS* 16 (1898): 46-49.

Note 6: "Dalhousie and Saint Andrews — A Coincidence." *Bulletin of the NHS* 16 (1898): 49-50.

Note 7: "On Halophytic Colonies in the Interior of New Brunswick." *Bulletin of the NHS* 16 (1898): 50-52.

Note 8: "Upon the Manner In Which the Bay of Fundy Rivers of New Brunswick Empty Into the Sea." *Bulletin of the NHS* 16 (1898): 52-54.

Note 9: "The Crayfish in New Brunswick." *Bulletin of the NHS* 16 (1898): 54.

Note 10: "The Marine Invertebrates of the Western Part of Bay Chaleur." *Bulletin of the NHS* 16 (1898): 55-56.

Note 11:   "A Natural History of New Brunswick Projected in 1771." *Bulletin of the NHS* 16 (1898): 56-57.

Note 12:   "On the Physiography of the Basin of the Mahood (Lepreau) Lakes." *Bulletin of the NHS* 16 (1898): 57-62.

Note 13:   "On New Heights in New Brunswick, Determined with Aneroid in 1897." *Bulletin of the NHS* 16 (1898): 62-63.

Note 14:   "On the Lack and Cost of a Topographical Survey of New Brunswick." *Bulletin of the NHS* 17 (1899): 122-24.

Note 15:   "Upon Natural Pavements and Their Possible Misinterpretation in Archaeology." *Bulletin of the NHS* 17 (1899): 124-25.

Note 16:   "On Attempts at Oyster Culture in Passamaquoddy Bay." *Bulletin of the NHS* 17 (1899): 125-26.

Note 17:   "On the Nature of the Mud In Our Many 'Mud Lakes'," *Bulletin of the NHS* 17 (1899): 126-27.

Note 18:   "Preliminary Outline of a Plan for a Study of the Precise Factors Determining the Features of New Brunswick Vegetation." *Bulletin of the NHS* 17 (1899): 127-30.

Note 19:   "On a Current Error as to the Location of (Nictor) Bald Mountain, Tobique." *Bulletin of the NHS* 17 (1899): 130-31.

Note 20:   "Upon Biological Opportunity in New Brunswick." *Bulletin of the NHS* 17 (1899): 131-34.

Note 21:   "Bibliography of the Freshwater Pearl Fishery in New Brunswick." *Bulletin of the NHS* 17 (1899): 134.

Note 22:   "Wind-Effects on Vegetation on the Isthmus of Chignecto." *Bulletin of the NHS* 17 (1899): 134-35.

Note 23:   "The Forestry Problem in New Brunswick." *Bulletin of the NHS* 18 (1899): 227-30.

Note 24:   "Cost of Topographical Survey of New Brunswick." *Bulletin of the NHS* 18 (1899): 230-31.

Note 25:   "What is the Highest Land in New Brunswick." *Bulletin of the NHS* 18 (1899): 231-33.

Note 26:   "On a Division of New Brunswick Into Physiographic Districts." *Bulletin of the NHS* 18 (1899): 233-36.

Note 27:   "On a Marked Browsing-Effect Observed Near St. Stephen." *Bulletin of the NHS* 18 (1899): 236-37.

Note 28:   "An Optical Illusion on the Peat Bogs of Charlotte County." *Bulletin of the NHS* 18 (1899): 237-38.

Note 29:   "On the Physiography of the Nictor Lake Region." *Bulletin of the NHS* 18 (1899): 238-48.

Note 30:   "Proposals for a Nomenclature of Unnamed New Brunswick Hills and Mountains." *Bulletin of the NHS* 18 (1899): 248-56.

Note 31:   "On Heights Determined with Aneroid in 1899." *Bulletin of the NHS* 18 (1899): 256-57.

Note 32:   "The Physiographic Origin of Our Portage Routes." *Bulletin of the NHS* 19 (1901): 313-14.

Note 33:   "The Physiographic History of the Nepisiguit River." *Bulletin of the NHS* 19 (1901): 314-19.

Note 34:   "On the Heights Above Sea Level of Nictor Lake and Neighboring Places." *Bulletin of the NHS* 19 (1901): 319-20.

Note 35:   "Peneplains and Monadnocks in New Brunswick." *Bulletin of the NHS* 19 (1901): 320-21.

Note 36:   "Further Suggestions Upon Nomenclature of Unnamed or Badly Named Places in New Brunswick." *Bulletin of the NHS* 19 (1901): 321-22.

Note 37:   "The Physiographic History of the Restigouche." *Bulletin of the NHS* 19 (1901): 322-23.

Note 38: "On the Use of Mineral or Divining Rods in New Brunswick." *Bulletin of the NHS* 19 (1901): 323-24.

Note 39: "On the Physiography of the Basin of the Negoot, or South Tobique Lakes." *Bulletin of the NHS* 19 (1901): 324-36.

Note 40: "On the Height of Nalaisk Mountain on the Serpentine." *Bulletin of the NHS* 19 (1901): 336-37.

Note 41: "On a Remarkable Crateriform Spring Near the Negoot Lakes." *Bulletin of the NHS* 19 (1901): 337-38.

Note 42: "On a Strange Position for a Peat-Bog." *Bulletin of the NHS* 19 (1901): 338-29.

Note 43: "Evidences of the Sinking of the Coast of New Brunswick." *Bulletin of the NHS* 19 (1901): 339-40.

Note 44: "On Forestry Literature Important for New Brunswick." *Bulletin of the NHS* 20 (1902): 427-28.

Note 45: "On the Physiographic History of the Tobique River." *Bulletin of the NHS* 20 (1902): 428-34.

Note 46: "Great Forest Fires in New Brunswick." *Bulletin of the NHS* 20 (1902): 434-35.

Note 47: "Measurements of Magnetic Dip in New Brunswick." *Bulletin of the NHS* 20 (1902): 435.

Note 48: "The Morphology of New Brunswick Waterfalls." *Bulletin of the NHS* 20 (1902): 436-40.

Note 49: "The Origin of the New Brunswick Peneplains." *Bulletin of the NHS* 20 (1902): 440-45.

Note 50: "The Physiographic History of the Miramichi River." *Bulletin of the NHS* 20 (1902): 445-50.

Note 51: "On a Lunar Rainbow Seen on Trowsers Lake." *Bulletin of the NHS* 20 (1902): 451.

Note 52: "On an Unusual Frost-Effect of 1901 on the Tobique." *Bulletin of the NHS* 20 (1902): 451.

Note 53: "On a Hypsometric Section Across Central New Brunswick." *Bulletin of the NHS* 20 (1902): 451-55.

Note 54: "On the Physiographic History of the Little Southwest Miramichi River." *Bulletin of the NHS* 20 (1902): 456-60.

Note 55: "On the Physiography of the Tuadook (Little Southwest Miramichi) Lake Region." *Bulletin of the NHS* 20 (1902): 461-68.

Note 56: "On the Physiography of the Milnagek (Island) Lake Basin." *Bulletin of the NHS* 20 (1902): 468-71.

Note 57: "Upon Sundry Natural Curiosities Said to Occur in New Brunswick." *Bulletin of the NHS* 21 (1903): 35-38.

Note 58: "Materials for a Study of Magnetic Variation in New Brunswick." *Bulletin of the NHS* 21 (1903): 38-40.

Note 59: "On the Types of River-Beds in New Brunswick." *Bulletin of the NHS* 21 (1903): 40-44.

Note 60: "On the Digdeguash Lake Basin." *Bulletin of the NHS* 21 (1903): 44-47.

Note 61: "A Preliminary Synopsis of the Grouping of the Vegetation (Phytogeography) of the Province of New Brunswick." *Bulletin of the NHS* 21 (1903): 47-60.

Note 62: "On New Heights in New Brunswick, Determined with Aneroid in 1902." *Bulletin of the NHS* 21 (1903): 60-65.

Note 63: "On the Physiography of the Adder Lake Stream Basin." *Bulletin of the NHS* 21 (1903): 65-71.

Note 64: "On the Physiography of the Graham Plains and Patchell Brook Region." *Bulletin of the NHS* 21 (1903): 71-75.

Note 65: "Upon Upsalquitch Lake, and Its Surroundings." *Bulletin of the NHS* 21 (1903): 75-82.

Note 66: "On Reported Occurrences of the Panther (Felis Concolor) in New Brunswick." *Bulletin of the NHS* 21 (1903): 82-86.

Note 67: "The Origin of Bald Head, Tobique." *Bulletin of the NHS* 21 (1903): 86-87.

Note 68: "The Nomenclature and Origin of the Geologist Range." *Bulletin of the NHS* 21 (1903): 87-88.

Note 69: "The Forestry Situation in New Brunswick." *Bulletin of the NHS* 21 (1903): 88-101.

Note 70: "Upon the Physiographic History of the Upsalquitch River." *Bulletin of the NHS* 22 (1904): 179-87.

Note 71: "On Some Peculiar Tree Forms Found in New Brunswick." *Bulletin of the NHS* 22 (1904): 187-89.

Note 72: "The Location of the Highest Land in New Brunswick." *Bulletin of the NHS* 22 (1904): 189-92.

Note 73: "The Physiographic History of the Oromocto River." *Bulletin of the NHS* 22 (1904): 192-200.

Note 74: "Notes on the Physiographic Origin of the Keswick River." *Bulletin of the NHS* 22 (1904): 200-202.

Note 75: "The Origin of the Fundian System of Rivers." *Bulletin of the NHS* 22 (1904): 202-12.

Note 76: "On New Aneroid Measurements in New Brunswick in 1903." *Bulletin of the NHS* 22 (1904): 212-15.

Note 77: "On the Physiography of the South Branch Nepisiguit." *Bulletin of the NHS* 22 (1904): 215-27.

Note 78: "On the Physiography of the Basin of the Northwest Miramichi." *Bulletin of the NHS* 22 (1904): 227.

Note 79: "On Additional Natural Curiosities Said to Occur in New Brunswick." *Bulletin of the NHS* 22 (1904): 236-40.

Note 80: "The Walrus in New Brunswick." *Bulletin of the NHS* 22 (1904): 240-41.

Note 81: "New Brunswick Animals and the Animal Romancers." *Bulletin of the NHS* 23 (1905): 299-304.

Note 82: "On Vegetable, or Burr, Balls from Little Kedron Lake." *Bulletin of the NHS* 23 (1905): 304-306.

Note 83: "A Measure of the Rate of Recession of the New Brunswick Coast Line." *Bulletin of the NHS* 23 (1905): 306-308.

Note 84: "New Aneroid Measurements in New Brunswick in 1904." *Bulletin of the NHS* 23 (1905): 308-11.

Note 85: "On the Physiographic Characteristics of the Renous River." *Bulletin of the NHS* 23 (1905): 311-20.

Note 86: "On the Physiographic Characteristics of the Southwest (Tuadook, or Crooked Deadwater) Branch of the Little Southwest Miramichi River." *Bulletin of the NHS* 23 (1905): 320-28.

Note 87: "On the Physiographic Characteristics of the Walkemik Basin (Upper North Branch of the Little Southwest Miramichi)." *Bulletin of the NHS* 23 (1905): 329-41.

Note 88: "On Geological Boundaries in the Tuadook–Walkemik Region." *Bulletin of the NHS* 23 (1905): 342-43.

Note 89: "On a Remarkable Noise Heard During a Forest Fire at Neguac." *Bulletin of the NHS* 24 (1906): 409-10.

Note 90: "On the Limits of the Great Fire of Miramichi of 1825." *Bulletin of the NHS* 24 (1906): 410-18.

Note 91: "On the Contour Map of New Brunswick." *Bulletin of the NHS* 24 (1906): 418-19.

Note 92: "The Fact Basis of the Fire (Or Phantom) Ship of Bay Chaleur." *Bulletin of the NHS* 24 (1906): 419-23.

Note 93: "The Origin of the Northumbrian System of Rivers." *Bulletin of the NHS* 24 (1906): 423-33.

Note 94: "The Physiographic Characteristics of the Tracadie River." *Bulletin of the NHS* 24 (1906): 433-43.

Note 95: "On the Height and Other Characters of Wilkinson Mountain." *Bulletin of the NHS* 24 (1906): 443-45.

Note 96: "Observations Upon the Weather of the Central Highlands." *Bulletin of the NHS* 24 (1906): 445-47.

Note 97: "On the Physical Geography of Miscou." *Bulletin of the NHS* 24 (1906): 447-62.

Note 98: "On Semi-Fossil Walrus Bones from Miscou and Elsewhere in New Brunswick." *Bulletin of the NHS* 24 (1906): 462-65.

Note 99: "On the Physiographic Characteristics of the North Pole Branch of the Little Southwest Miramichi River." *Bulletin of the NHS* 24 (1906): 465-73.

Note 100: "The Recognition and Utilization of the Plateau Structure of Interior NB." *Bulletin of the NHS* 24 (1906): 473-74.

Note 101: "On the Physiographic Characteristics of the Tabusintac River." *Bulletin of the NHS* 25 (1907): 519-24.

Note 102: "On the Physiographic Characteristics of the Pokemouche and Saint Simon Rivers." *Bulletin of the NHS* 25 (1907): 524-56.

Note 103: "A Downward-Forking Brook Near Nictor Lake." *Bulletin of the NHS* 25 (1907): 526.

Note 104: "On the Physiographic Characteristics of the Lower North (Or Apskqu) Branch of the Little Southwest Miramichi." *Bulletin of the NHS* 25 (1907): 527-32.

Note 105: "On the Square Forks of the Sevogle and Their 'Interglacial' Testimony." *Bulletin of the NHS* 25 (1907): 533-37.

Note 106: "On the Physiographic Characteristics of the Sevogle River." *Bulletin of the NHS* 25 (1907): 537-46.

Note 107: "On the Physiographic Characteristics of Portage and Fox Islands, Miramichi." *Bulletin of the NHS* 26 (1908): 17-22.

Note 108: "The Physical Geography of the North Shore Sand Islands." *Bulletin of the NHS* 26 (1908): 22-29.

Note 109: "The Height of the Highest New Brunswick Waterfall." *Bulletin of the NHS* 26 (1908): 29-30.

Note 110: "On the Occurrence of the Wolf In New Brunswick." *Bulletin of the NHS* 26 (1908): 30-35.

Note 111: "On the Fundamental Construction of the Central Highlands of New Brunswick." *Bulletin of the NHS* 26 (1908): 35-36.

Note 112: "On the Psychological Basis of New Brunswick Sea-serpents." *Bulletin of the NHS* 26 (1908): 36-39.

Note 113: "The Physiographic Characteristics of the Upper Main Southwest Miramichi River." *Bulletin of the NHS* 27 (1909): 85-104.

Note 114: "On an Indispensable Pre-requisite to a Successful Forestry Policy for New Brunswick." *Bulletin of the NHS* 27 (1909): 104-107.

Note 115: "The Highest New Brunswick Waterfalls." *Bulletin of the NHS* 27 (1909): 107-108.

Note 116: "A Test of the Accuracy of Aneroid Measurements in Interior New Brunswick." *Bulletin of the NHS* 27 (1909): 108-109.

Note 117: "On The Physical Geography of the Muniac Stream." *Bulletin of the NHS* 28 (1910): 199-201.

Note 118: "On The Physiographic Characteristics of Cains River." *Bulletin of the NHS* 28 (1910): 201-10.

Note 118a: "Supplement To Note 118: The Ancient Indian Portage from Cains River to the Gaspereau." *Bulletin of the NHS* 28 (1910): 210-16.

Note 119: "An Absolute Measure of the Rate of Recession of the New Brunswick Coast Line." *Bulletin of the NHS* 28 (1910): 216-18.

Note 120: "On the Physical Geography of Bartholomew River." *Bulletin of the NHS* 29 (1911): 321-25.

Note 121: "A Preliminary Study of the Saxby Gale." *Bulletin of the NHS* 29 (1911): 325-30.

Note 122: "On the Duration of Open Water on the Saint John River." *Bulletin of the NHS* 29 (1911): 330-32.

Note 123: "On the Physiographic Characteristics of the Renous Lakes." *Bulletin of the NHS* 29 (1911): 333-37.

Note 124: "On Temperature Measurements of New Brunswick Springs." *Bulletin of the NHS* 30 (1913): 419-21.

Note 125: "On the Physiographic Characteristics of the Gaspereau (Sunbury-Queens) Rivers." *Bulletin of the NHS* 30 (1913): 421-29.

Note 125a: "Supplement to Note 125: The Ancient Indian Portage from Gaspereau to Cains River." *Bulletin of the NHS* 30 (1913): 429-34.

Note 126: "The Physiographic Characteristics of Salmon River (Queens-Kent)." *Bulletin of the NHS* 30 (1913): 434-44.

Note 126a: "Supplement to Note 126: The Ancient Indian Portage from Salmon River to the Richibucto." *Bulletin of the NHS* 30 (1913): 444-49.

Note 127: "On the Stability of the New Brunswick Coast." *Bulletin of the NHS* 30 (1913): 450-51.

Note 128: "Further Data Upon the Rate of Recession of the Coast Line of New Brunswick." *Bulletin of the NHS* 31 (1914): 1-5.

Note 129: "The Physiographic Characteristics of Lake Stream, Queens-Kent." *Bulletin of the NHS* 31 (1914): 5-8.

Note 130: "On the Physiographic Characteristics of Coal Creek, Queens County." *Bulletin of the NHS* 31 (1914): 8-11.

Note 131: "On the Physiographic Characteristics of the Washademoak-Canaan River." *Bulletin of the NHS* 31 (1914): 12-23.

Note 131a: "Supplement to Note 131: The Ancient Indian Portages from the Washademoak to Adjacent Waters." *Bulletin of the NHS* 31 (1914): 23-34.

Note 132: "The Remarkable Twelve-Hour Tides of Buctouche." *Bulletin of the NHS* 31 (1914): 35-37.

Note 133: "The Gordon Falls, and Associated Gorges, on Pollett River." *Bulletin of the NHS* 32 (1917): 105-11.

Note 134: "The Great Snowstorm of June 5, 1914, in Central New Brunswick." *Bulletin of the NHS* 32 (1917): 111-13.

Note 135: "The Movement of the Head of Tide on New Brunswick Rivers." *Bulletin of the NHS* 32 (1917): 113-25.

Note 136: "The West Branch of the South Branch of Nepisiguit, and the Central Plateau." *Bulletin of the NHS* 32 (1917): 125-32.

Note 137: "The Physiographic Axes of New Brunswick." *Bulletin of the NHS* 32 (1917): 132-33.

Note 138: "A Postglacial Gorge Sixty Years of Age." *Bulletin of the NHS* 32 (1917): 133-34.

Notes

Laying the Groundwork

1   Webster, *William Francis Ganong Memorial*, 3.

2   Susan B. Ganong's contribution in *William Francis Ganong Memorial*, 7.

3   My research suggests that there is no New Brunswick stream named Clinch, but the NB Land Grant Plan reference map GP No. 164 indicates property belonging to people of that name. The only stream running through that property was named Perch, so I believe that this is the stream Ganong and his uncles fished.

4   "Ganong Field Trip Notes," *New Brunswick Journals*, William Francis Ganong fonds, F455, New Brunswick Museum (hereafter cited as Ganong fonds). The NB Museum rewrote a small portion of Ganong's field notes.

5   Webster, *William Francis Ganong Memorial*, 5.

6   Jean Ganong died in 1920. Ganong then married Anna Hobbett, his assistant in the botany department at Smith College, and fathered the first of two children at the age of sixty.

7   Clayden, "William Francis Ganong," *NBM News* (Fall 1991), 2.

8   Ganong, note 23: "The Forestry Problem in New Brunswick," 227.

Chapter 1: Learning to Lead

1   Clayden, "William Francis Ganong," 1.

2   Ganong, "Camping on the St. Croix."

3   Ganong, "The Meaning of the Day," 25.

4   Ganong, "Camping on the St. Croix."

5   Ganong, "The Zoology of the Invertebrate Animals of Passamaquoddy Bay," 89.

6   Ganong, "Looking for Old Indian Encampment on Minister Island."

Chapter 2: Science and History

1 Ganong, "Returning from Squatook."

2 In subsequent summers, Ganong would travel back many times to the Tobique River, using it as a gateway to the central highlands and his explorations of the interior of the province.

Chapter 3: Romantic and Picturesque

1 Ganong, note 4: "On the Color of the Water in New Brunswick Rivers," 44.

2 Hay, "The Restigouche," 12. Dr. Philip Cox (natural scientist, educator, and author) and Mr. John Brittain (botanist), members of the Natural History Society of New Brunswick.

3 Hay, "The Restigouche," 14.

4 Ibid., 16.

5 Ganong, "Restigouche Trip with George Upham Hay." I am unsure why Ganong chose not to use the Waagan Brook, commonly known as the beginning of the traditional portage route from the Restigouche to the Grand River.

6 Hay, "The Restigouche," 21.

7 Ganong, note 37: "The Physiographic History of the Restigouche," 37.

8 Hay, "The Restigouche," 28.

9 Ganong, note 5: "On the Heights of New Brunswick Hills," 46.

10 Ganong, note 4: "On the Color of the Water in New Brunswick Rivers," 44.

Chapter 4: A Sense of Adventure

1 Ganong named the lakes in honour of the deputy surveyor for Charlotte County William Mahood, whose work charting the geography of Charlotte County he admired.

2 Webster, *William Francis Ganong Memorial*, 5.

3 Ganong, note 12: "On the Physiography of the Basin of the Mahood (Lepreau) Lakes," 61.

4 Ibid., 57.

5 Ibid., 60.

6 Ganong, note 8: "Upon the Manner In Which the Bay of Fundy Rivers of New Brunswick Empty into the Sea," 52.

Chapter 5: The Complicated River

1 Ganong, note 33: "The Physiographic History of the Nepisiguit River," 319.

2 Ganong refers to the settlement at Nictau and the lake as 'Nictor' in his reports.

3 Before construction of a hydro dam at the Tobique Narrows in the 1950s, anglers revered the river for its salmon fishing.

4 Ganong, note 33: "The Physiographic History of The Nepisiguit River," 314.

5 Ibid.

6 Ganong, note 29: "On the Physiography of the Nictor Lake Region," 238.

7 Ganong, note 29: "On the Physiography of the Nictor Lake Region," 240.

8 Ibid., 243.

9 Ganong, note 25: "What is the Highest Land in New Brunswick?" 233.

10 Ganong, "Tobique to the Nepisiguit Fieldtrip with Mauran Furbish."

11 Ganong, note 33: "The Physiographic History of the Nepisiguit River," 315.

12 Ganong, "Tobique to the Nepisiguit Fieldtrip with Mauran Furbish."

13 Ganong, note 33: "The Physiographic History of the Nepisiguit River," 317.

14 Nepisiguit Falls was also known as "Great" and "Grand." Today the section of river between the narrows and the waterfalls is much tamer, thanks to the influence of the electric-power generation dam at the falls.

15 These are features one would usually expect to find in the upper reaches of a river, but in the case of the Nepisiguit River, they occur almost at its confluence with Chaleur Bay.

16 Ganong, note 23: "The Forestry Problem in New Brunswick," 229.

17 Presented to the Natural History Society of New Brunswick on December 5, 1899.

18 Ganong, note 29: "On the Physiography of the Nictor Lake Region," 247.

Chapter 6: A Sportsman's Paradise

1 Ganong, note 39: "On the Physiography of the Basin of the Negoot, or South Tobique Lakes," 326.

2 Ganong, note 45: "On the Physiographic History of the Tobique River," 434.

3 A peneplain is a broad, mostly flat expanse of land formed during the final stage of erosion by mature rivers; the Central Highlands peneplain is more than 450 metres above sea level.

4 Ganong, note 39: "On the Physiography of the Basin of the Negoot, or South Tobique Lakes," 327-28.

5 Ibid., 331.

6 Ibid., 330.

7 Ganong, note 41: "On a Remarkable Crateriform Spring near the Negoot Lakes," 337.

8 Ganong, note 40: "On the Height of Nalaisk Mountain on the Serpentine," 336.

9 Ganong, note 42: "On a Strange Position for a Peat-Bog," 338.

10 Ibid., 339.

Chapter 7: The Primeval Wilderness

1 Ganong, note 53: "On a Hypsometric Section Across Central New Brunswick," 451.

2 Ibid., 453.

3 Ganong, note 51: "On a Lunar Rainbow Seen on Trowsers Lake," 451.

4 Ganong, note 56: "On the Physiography of the Milnagek (Island) Lake Basin," 471.

5 Ibid., 451.

6 The NB Woodsman's Museum in Boiestown has a replica of one of Braithwaite's hunting camps.

7 Ganong, note 55: "On the Physiography of the Tuadook (Little Southwest Miramichi) Lake Region," 463.

8 Ganong, note 54: "On the Physiographic History of the Little Southwest Miramichi River," 457.

9 Ibid.

Chapter 8: Uncharted Country

1   Ganong, note 63: "On the Physiography of the Adder Lake Stream Basin," 65.

2   Ibid., 71.

3   Ganong, note 64: "On the Physiography of the Graham Plains and Patchell Brook Region," 72.

4   Ibid., 73.

5   Ibid., 74.

6   Ganong, note 70: "Upon the Physiographic History of the Upsalquitch River," 181.

7   Ganong, note 65: "Upon Upsalquitch Lake, and Its Surroundings," 77.

8   An aide-de-camp with General Wolfe during the Seven Year War, DesBarres created a large collection of maps, charts, and sketches of North America.

9   Ganong, note 70: "Upon the Physiographic History of the Upsalquitch River," 182.

10 Ibid., 185.

Chapter 9: A Nomadic Life

1   Susan B. Ganong's contribution in *William Francis Ganong Memorial*, J.C. Webster, ed., 7.

2   Ganong, note 73: "The Physiographic History of the Oromocto River," 192.

3   Ibid., 196-97.

4   Behind Fredericton Junction's historic Currie House lie a small valley and brook. I made my way to what Ganong's observations led me to believe was the original course of the river, starting at the valley's eastern end and proceeding westward to emerge at the river just below the railway bridge crossing the North Branch. Indeed, this certainly appears to be the preglacial path for the river.

5   Ganong, note 73: "The Physiographic History of the Oromocto River," 198.

6   Ibid., 199.

7   Ganong, note 74: "Notes On the Physiographic Origin of the Keswick River," 200.

8   Ibid., 201.

9   Ganong, "Field Trip with Arthur Pierce from the South Branch Nepisiguit to the Northwest Miramichi."

10 Ganong, note 77: "On the Physiography of the South Branch Nepisiguit," 215.

11 Ibid., 216.

12 Ibid., 217-18.

13 Arthur Pierce journal, August 18, 1903.

14 Ganong, note 77: "On the Physiography of the South Branch Nepisiguit," 218.

15 Ibid., 223.

16 Arthur Pierce journal, August 28, 1903.

17 Arthur Pierce journal, August 29, 1903.

18 Ganong, note 78: "On the Physiography of the Basin of the Northwest Miramichi," 232-33. I ventured down into the gorge in August 2012 to photograph and experience first-hand the spectacle Ganong described. In September of the same year I visited the gorge at Grand Falls. I cannot concur with Ganong's observation. The gorge, although awe-inspiring, does not compare with the grandeur of the gorge at Grand Falls.

19 Arthur Pierce journal, September 4, 1903.

Chapter 10: The Ancient Land

1 Ganong, note 77: "On the Physiography of the South Branch Nepisiguit," 223.

2 Ganong, note 86: "On the Physiographic Characteristics of the Southwest (Tuadook, or Crooked Deadwater) Branch of the Little Southwest Miramichi River," 327.

3 Ganong, note 87: "On the Physiographic Characteristics of the Walkemik Basin (Upper North Branch of the Little Southwest Miramichi," 329.

4 Ibid.

5 Arthur Pierce journal, July 14, 1904.

6 Ibid., July 25, 1904.

7 Ibid., July 30, 1904.

8 Ganong, note 87: "On the Physiographic Characteristics of the Walkemik Basin (Upper North Branch of the Little Southwest Miramichi)," 333.

9 Ibid., 321.

10 Ibid., 328.

11 Arthur Pierce journal, August 20, 1904.

12 Ganong, note 85: "On the Physiographic Characteristics of the Renous River," 317. Ganong mistakenly named the Little North Branch as the Little South Branch. The Little South Branch is a tributary of the South Branch Renous River which does not have its headwaters in North Renous Lake.

13 Arthur Pierce journal, August 24, 1904.

14 Ibid., August 25, 1904.

15 Ganong, note 119: "An Absolute Measure of the Rate of Recession of the New Brunswick Coast Line," 216.

16 Ganong, note 86: "On the Physiographic Characteristics of the Southwest (Tuadook, or Crooked Deadwater) Branch of the Little Southwest Miramichi River," 323.

Chapter 11: Through Darkest New Brunswick

1 Ganong, note 127: "On the Stability of the New Brunswick Coast," 450.

2 Ganong, note 99: "On the Physiographic Characteristics of the North Pole Branch of the Little Southwest Miramichi River," 465.

3 Skunk Lake is now called Hatch Lake.

4 Today, this area is known as the Christmas Mountains. Its location in the central highlands of the province, remote from any settlement, meant that few people at the turn of the century knew of it.

5 Ganong, note 99: "On the Physiographic Characteristics of the North Pole Branch of the Little Southwest Miramichi River," 469.

6 Accompanied by Terry Gallant, I hiked out to Half Moon Lake and then to the location indicated on Ganong's map. We found several small broken falls but none of substantial height. A proliferation of downfalls made trekking down in the ravine difficult.

7 Arthur Pierce journal, July 22, 1905.

8 Ibid., July 25, 1905. My own measurements revealed that the major pitch in that series of three waterfalls is just over 12 metres (approximately 40 feet).

9 Ibid., July 25, 1905.

10 Ibid., July 27, 1905.

11 Ibid.

12 Ibid., July 28 1905. "Cruiser" was a common term for a forester examining a stand of timber for its potential value.

13 Ibid., August 4, 1905.

14 Ganong, note 108: "The Physical Geography of the North Shore Sand Islands," 22.

15 Ganong, note 97: "On the Physical Geography of Miscou," 447.

16 Ibid.

17 Ibid.

18 Arthur Pierce journal, August 17, 1905. I visited Miscou and Lameque, the ancestral home of my grandparents, in 2011 and 2012. The surnames Ward and Poirier are prevalent in the local cemeteries and history of the islands. Of the many places photographed for this book, Miscou was one of my favourites.

Chapter 12: Strikingly Wild

1 Ganong, note 106: "On the Physiographic Characteristics of the Sevogle River," 537.

2 Ganong, note 104: "On the Physiographic Characteristics of the Lower North (Or Apskwa) Branch of the Little Southwest Miramichi," 527.

3 Ganong, note 61: "A Preliminary Synopsis of the Grouping of the Vegetation (Phytogeography) of the Province of New Brunswick," 48.

4 Ganong, note 104: "On the Physiographic Characteristics of the Lower North (Or Apskwa) Branch of the Little Southwest Miramichi," 528.

5 Arthur Pierce journal, July 16, 1906.

6 Arthur Pierce journal, July 17, 1906. In October 2012, Terry Gallant and I drove out to within half a kilometre of the lake and then followed a trail out to the lake. A thin layer of snow and a chill in the air made the late-morning hike enjoyable. Freeze Lake in reality is made up of two distinct bodies of water. The Ganong image is of the southern lake and mine is of the northern lake.

7 Ibid., July 20, 1906.

8 Ibid.

9 Ganong, note 106: "On the Physiographic Characteristics of the Sevogle River," 543.

10 Ibid., 545.

11 Arthur Pierce journal, July 27, 1906.

12 Lumbermen commonly blasted narrow channels with dynamite so timber could flow past, which explains the difference in the height of the falls in these pictures.

13 Ganong, note 105: "On the Square Forks of the Sevogle and Their 'Interglacial' Testimony," 533.

14 Ibid., 534.

15 Ibid., 534-35.

Chapter 13: A Challenging Puzzle

1 Webster, *William Francis Ganong Memorial*, 3.

2 Ganong, note 113: "The Physiographic Characteristics of the Upper Main Southwest Miramichi River," 85.

3 Ibid. The entire river is known as the Southwest Miramichi. I suspect Ganong used the term "Upper" to delineate it from the section below Boiestown and the term "Main" to delineate it from the Little Southwest Miramichi.

4 Ganong, note 113: "The Physiographic Characteristics of the Upper Main Southwest Miramichi River," 86.

5 Arthur Pierce journal, July 24, 1908.

6 Ibid., July 28, 1908.

7 Ibid., July 29, 1908.

8 Ibid., August 8, 1908.

9 Ganong, note 115: "The Highest New Brunswick Waterfalls," 108. Although Ganong wrote "Merry Pitcher" the actual name is Mary Pitcher.

10 Arthur Pierce journal, August 9, 1908.

11 Burke, *Historical Earthquakes Felt In New Brunswick*, 460.

Chapter 14: Unfinished Business

1 Susan B. Ganong's contribution in *William Francis Ganong Memorial*, J.C. Webster, ed., 9.

2 Ganong, note 115: "The Highest New Brunswick Waterfalls," 107.

3 Ganong, note 118: "On the Physiographic Characteristics of Cains River," 201.

4 Ibid., 206.

5 Ibid., 209.

6 Ibid., 210.

7 Ganong, note 118a: "Supplement to Note 118," 210.

8 Ganong, note 118: "On the Physiographic Characteristics of Cains River," 203.

9 Ganong, note 118a: "Supplement to Note 118," 213.

10 Ibid.

11 Ibid., 211. In November 2012, Terry Gallant and I hiked the freshly cut portage trail to the Cains River. Moving downriver, we looked for the Portage Rock as indicated on the Ganong map. Sure enough, across the river, approximately 200 metres from the trail, is a large flat rock lying on its edge that fits Ganong's description.

12 Ibid., 214.

Chapter 15: Historical Significance

1 Ganong, note 125: "On the Physiographic Characteristics of the Gaspereau (Sunbury-Queens) Rivers," 421.

2 Ganong, note 32: "The Physiographic Origin of Our Portage Routes," 314.

3 Ganong, note 118a: "Supplement To Note 118," 216.

4 Ganong, note 125a: "Supplement To Note 125," 431.

5 In 2008, Kevin Silliker, Tim Humes, and Robert Doyle started the restoration of six ancient portage trails on behalf of Canoe Kayak NB (CKNB), using research by Doyle that was largely based on the immense work of Ganong. The trails were chosen for their historical importance, their representation of the main rivers of New Brunswick, and Crown Land access. Just as the ancient portage trails connected watersheds, this ongoing restoration project connects the past and the present.

6 Ganong, note 125a: "Supplement to Note 125," 434.

7 Today, the Renous Lakes are called the Kennedy Lakes.

8 Ganong, note 119: "An Absolute Measure of the Rate of Recession of the New Brunswick Coast Line," 217.

9 Ibid., 216.

Chapter 16: The Land of Meadows and Water

1 Susan B. Ganong's contribution in *William Francis Ganong Memorial,* J.C. Webster, ed., 9.

2 Ganong, note 125: "On the Physiographic Characteristics of the Gaspereau (Sunbury-Queens) Rivers," 421.

3 Ibid.

4 Ibid., 425.

5 Ganong, note 126: "The Physiographic Characteristics of Salmon River (Queens-Kent)," 436-37.

6 Ibid., 437.

7 Ibid., 438.

8 Ganong, note 126: "The Physiographic Characteristics of Salmon River (Queens-Kent)," 440.

9 Ganong, note 129: "The Physiographic Characteristics of Lake Stream, Queens-Kent," 6.

Chapter 17: The Land of Canaan

1 Ganong, note 131: "On the Physiographic Characteristics of the Washademoak-Canaan River," 12.

2 Ganong, note 131a: "Supplement to Note 131," 25.

3 Ganong, note 131: "On the Physiographic Characteristics of the Washademoak-Canaan River," 15.

4 Ibid., 17.

5 Ganong, note 131a: "Supplement to Note 131," 25-26.

6 Ganong, note 131: "On the Physiographic Characteristics of the Washademoak-Canaan River," 19. Laminated argillites are layers of fine-grained sedimentary rock, intermediate between shale and slate.

7 Ibid., 20.

Sundry Items

1 Ganong, note 66: "On Reported Occurrences of the Panther (Felis Concolor) in New Brunswick," 83.

2 Ganong, note 81: "New Brunswick Animals and the Animal Romancers."

3 Ganong, note 82: "On Vegetable, or Burr, Balls from Little Kendron Lake," 304.

4 Ganong, note 90: "On The Limits of the Great Fire of Miramichi of 1825," 410.

5 Ganong, note 92: "The Fact Basis of the Fire (or Phantom) Ship of Bay Chaleur," 420.

6 Ganong, note 110: "On the Occurrence of the Wolf in New Brunswick," 31.

7 Gyles, *Memoirs of Odd Adventures, Strange Deliverances, Etc.*

Selected Bibliography

Burke, Kenneth B.S. *Historical Earthquakes Felt in New Brunswick (1764, 1811-1960)*. Fredericton: Sandler Geophysical, 2009.

Clayden, S. "William Francis Ganong." *NBM News* (Fall 1991).

Dashwood, Richard Lewes. *Chiploquorgan: or, Life by the Campfire in Dominion of Canada and Newfoundland*. 1872. Canadian Reprint Series, no. 2. Fredericton: Saint Anne's Press, 1979.

Ganong, W.F. *Champlain's Island: An Expanded Edition of Ste. Croix (Dochet) Island*. Saint John: The New Brunswick Museum, 2003.

Gyles, John. *Memoirs of Odd Adventures, Strange Deliverances, Etc., in the Captivity of John Gyles, Esq., Commander of the Garrison on Saint George River, in the District of Maine*. Boston, 1736. Reprinted Cincinnati: Spiller & Gates, 1869.

Hay, G.U. "The Restigouche — With Notes Especially on Its Flora" *Bulletin of the Natural History Society of New Brunswick* 16 (1896): 21.

Heuer, Karsten. *Walking the Big Wild: From Yellowstone to the Yukon on the Grizzly Bear's Trail*. Toronto: McClelland & Stewart, 2003.

New Brunswick Museum. "William Francis Ganong's field trips around the province of New Brunswick." Accessed April 8, 2011. http://website.nbm-mnb.ca/CAIN/english/william_ganong.

Webster, J.C., ed. *William Francis Ganong Memorial*. Saint John: New Brunswick Museum, 1942.

Index

Nicholas Guitard is the photographer and author of two books about waterfalls. His *Waterfalls of New Brunswick: A Guide* is widely used by nature enthusiasts and families who wish to explore natural beauty of New Brunswick. His interest in William Francis Ganong grew out of an appreciation of Ganong's pioneering work as a naturalist and a shared affection for their province of birth.